Testimonials

"Susmita has written a beautiful and powerful book. It integrates the Buddhist path with our pressing real issues of living well together in wellness, justice, and true harmony."

-Dr. Larry Ward, Zen teacher, cofounder and executive director of The Lotus Institute, Pataskala, Ohio

"Susmita's book is an inspiring journey, with deep and useful Dharma practices throughout. May her story and practices inspire women from all over the world."

-Amita Schmidt, LCSW, Meditation Teacher and Author of Dipa Ma

"Susmita Barua has written a book of guidance on the path to deeper self-knowledge and ultimately towards freedom from the bondage of our own confusion. Ironically it is often an inspiration to read of others' struggles and achievements on the spiritual path, and we are grateful to the author for sharing the fruits of her insight and practice so that we can go forward with confidence. It is always helpful to have a well sign-posted road to follow."

-Ven. Tenzin Palmo, Founding Teacher of DGL Nunnery, Author of The Heroic Heart, who lived 12 years in a Himalayan cave.

Susmita Barua has given all of humanity a great treasure of spiritual wisdom and guidance. She writes, "This higher dimensional pure energy of peace, unconditional love, and bliss can catalyze the social and collective awakening of many." Her book is filled with that energy, and will no doubt contribute to the great work of the awakening of humanity.

-Marc Allen, Publisher, New World Library,
and Author of The Magical Path

"In *Awakening With Ease*, Susmita (Acharya Nava) offers a practical example of spiritual awakening. But note that *practical* does not mean *linear*. Through spirals of personal experience, introduction to Buddhist principles, and advice for the seeker who knows there must be something more, Susmita draws the reader ever closer to her own awakening through wise attention to the birthplace of wisdom."

-Rev. Christie Bates LPC (Acharya Passatininna), author
and contemplative at The Beautiful Human School

"In her wonderful book, *Awakening with Ease*, Susmita shares her personal journey of Awakening into a greater embrace of Buddhism to encourage others to do the same. A seeker and mystic from childhood, she recounts marvelous and magical experiences and shares deep insights to inspire us all to discover and embrace the Divinity of who we are. She encourages her readers to "... bring wonder, curiosity, and inquiry as you read this book." When you do, I know that you will be generously rewarded!"

-Paul Hoyt, best-selling author of *The Practice of
Awakening II: The First Light of Joy*

"Simultaneously spiritual and pragmatic, Awakening with Ease cuts to the heart of discovering and living from our deepest sense of humanity, both individually and collectively. This volume is a synthesis of mindfulness practice, Buddhist thought, and insights gained from the author's experiences within inequitable social and professional contexts. As a storyteller, Barua's writing style is literal, allegorical, and instructional in just the right portions... she mindfully interweaves the many threads we will all encounter as we search both inward and outward for our sense of place in this world."

-Jonathan Reynolds, CEO at Mindful Life, Mindful Work, Inc.

"As a long-time peace activist and teacher, I see Awareness with Ease (AWE) as welcome guidance toward a kinder and more compassionate world. Using stories from her own experience, Susmita takes readers through the tenets of the Buddha's Eight (or Ten) Fold Path, demonstrating how greater awareness leads to an awake and enriched life. This path calls for wise livelihood, for self, others and the environment and giving up narrow identity and self-view. Peace, awareness, and wise attention cultivated within ripples outward."

-Rebecca Claire Glasscock, PhD, Professor Emerita, Geography and Peace Studies, Bluegrass Community and Technical College, Lexington KY

AWAKENING
WITH
EASE

A Simple Direct Path for Wise Women Leaders,
Mindful Entrepreneurs, Immigrants, Minorities, and Seekers

Plus Wise Attention to the New Paradigm

SUSMITA BARUA
(ACHARYA NAVA)

ISBN: 978-1-64184-878-7 (paperback)
ISBN: 978-1-64184-877-0 (hardback)
ISBN: 978-1-64184-879-4 (ebook)

To the brave ones who commit to
Awaken With Ease

Noble ancestors: Ven. Kripasaran and Dipa Ma Barua
Wise parents: Netra Ranjan and Manjusree Barua

Table of Contents

Acknowledgements. xiii

Foreword by Ven. Lekshe xv

Introduction xix

    Why awakening is important now xxv
    In this book you'll discover. xxvii
    How to use this book and what to expect xxix
    A Quick Hello xxxii
    The AWE method: how and why it works. xxxiv
    My short story. xxxvi
    The myths of spiritual awakening xxxvii

Part I

Chapter 1: My Memoir in a Few Mustard Seeds. 3

    The most important things in the book 11
    More on Awakening (AWE). 13
    The great turning inward. 15
    Beginner's mind 16
    Spiritual urgency of samvega. 18
    Breakdown to breakthrough 20
    Recollection of past grief and joy 21
    Life as an immigrant in the US 22
    Awakening With Ease: going deeper 23
    Awakening from the dream of samsara. 24
    Rohitassa and other suttas 28
    Process of inquiry and intention. 29
    Longer story as an immigrant to the US 31

Marriage, Work and Family. 32
Myth of happiness. 33
Why I needed to write this. 34
Why this book and who it is for 36
How this book helps you as a leader 41
What's going to happen in the world 42

Chapter 2: Know Your Why and Your Story 47
Here's why this is important 47
What is the benefit and for whom. 48
Why it is important. 48
A little history and language on enlightenment. 49
Bridging enlightened society, self and citizens. 50
What is the benefit and for whom. 51
Benefits of awakening (enlightenment) 51
A simple foundation for happiness 54
Gift from a stranger 56
Learning within family 57
Dream of hunger, pain, and death 58
Enigma of eldest son (sibling) 59
Change is sudden and unexpected 60
Insights from travel and pilgrimage 61

Part II

Chapter 3: Alive 67
From depression and grief to aliveness now. 70
Presence in daily chores. 73
Samvega to pasada is possible 75
Song of the universe. 76
Cosmic AWE 77
Making space for the sacred in daily life. 78

Chapter 4: Ask 81
Time for deep thinking (contemplation) 82
Let go of worldly preoccupation 83

Contemplation on death and life 85
What is the ancient Arya way of mindful living 86
Acinteyya - four imponderables 87
Dhamma vicaya: investigation of dhamma 88

Chapter 5: Abandon 89
Transforming tanha to chanda 92
Ignorance of the Law of Causation
    (paṭiccasamuppāda) 96
From ayoniso to yoniso manasikara 97
From pamada to appamada 102
From form to formless and sunyata 104

Chapter 6: Accept 107
Unwholesome to wholesome states 109
Healing with four divine emotions 113
Buddhist ethics: the ends do not justify the means 113
Life's great blessings (Mahamangala Sutta) 115
Embracing our human emotional journey 117
Map of Human Emotion, Psychological
    and Spiritual Growth 118

Chapter 7: Aware 123
Mindful meditation (samma-sati and samadhi) 125
Bahiya's awakening 130
The seven awakening factors 131
Relationship of Sati and Seven Factors 133
Samatha and vipassana go together 134
The Middle Way to End Ignorance 136
Three Marks of Existence 139
Kamma: old, new, and its ending 140
Overflowing with merit (punna) 142

Chapter 8: Awaken 143
Awakening from the illusion to reality 144
Right worldview and Intention 147
What this means to you 148

Metta as the base of mindfulness 150
Bodhicitta resolve 151
Going beyond fear, doubt, and identity-view 153
The Four Stages of Awakening and the Ten Fetters . . 154
Ten Fetters 155
Thirty-one planes of existence 156
Power of enlightened consciousness 158
From ignorance to knowledge of liberation 159

Part III

Chapter 9: Conclusion 165

Conventional education 167
More on nibbana (unbinding) 169
Sangha of AWE Circles 171
Reflections on a vision for the planet 173
Spontaneous engagements 174
Effects of awakening 175
The New Earth Paradigm 176
Guardians of true dharma 178
AWE circles 180

Bibliography 189

Acknowledgements

This precious human life would not be possible without the support of this beautiful Earth we walk on each day, all the elements, and the sun and moon. So contemplating their qualities I bow to them often. Also our bodies are made of stardust. Every atom of oxygen in our lungs, carbon in our muscles, calcium in our bones, and iron in our blood was created inside a star before the Earth was born. Our connection to the greater cosmos, source of all life and non-self is nothing short of an imponderable miracle capable of awakening joy, wonder and AWE, if we can only learn to slow down, pause, breathe, reflect, and remember!

I bow to my wise ancestors whose perseverance and generosity prepared the ground for me to wake up in this life. Deep love for my parents who nurtured, cleaned and fed me and my siblings day by day, moment by moment when we were incapable of doing so. This includes over 3500+ times of cleaning nappies in first 3 years. As I grow older this recognition puts me in gratitude mode. I bow to all, whose labor of love produced and prepared the food and drink on my table, delivered my paper mails, paved the roads, taught me dhamma chanda, drove me to my destination, worked together in harmony, listened with respect, or welcomed me with their kind eyes or a smile.

I like to acknowledge all my spiritual and nature friends who held the mirror of wakeful presence, compassion, natural humor, inspiration, clear mind, and joy momentarily to wake me up when I was conflicted, afraid, distracted and blind-sided. Fortunately there is always help available if we are looking. Taking a long pause of over a year and half allowed me to finish this book that got interrupted three times before in past twelve years. I am grateful to all who took my book interview, and all those who took the time to read and send a testimonial. Special thanks to my writing coach and author Ben Gioia for helping me put structure to the book, editor Chris O'Byrne for putting his final refinements, and Debbie O'Byrne for the elegant cover design.

My gratitude to Lexington Shambhala and Buddhist Peace Fellowship where I got to learn about and practice my spiritual warriorship to bring the gift of feminine principle in Dhamma, do some engaged grassroot work of peace and justice and mindful economics under the radar. I am most grateful for finding my spiritual home, non-sectarian sisterhood and mentors in the Sakyadhita International Association of Buddhist Women and the Alliance for bhikkhunis; both did not require any formal Buddhist teaching credential for me to speak, teach and serve in leadership capacities.

I was lucky to have the access to a Dharmacharya program for non-monastic lay people initiated by Venerables Pannadipa and Pannavati of the Embracing Simplicity Contemplative Order. Instead of naming two dozen monastics and lay teachers who inspired me personally to gently embody Dhamma, I will name a few spiritual friends. They are Ven. Bhikkhu Jnanajagat, Dipa Ma, Dipa, Lea Schultz, Bhante Nanda, Bhikkhuni Tathaaloka, Bhikkhu Bodhi, and late Ven. Pannadipa Bhikkhu, who really encouraged me to follow my heart and wanted to see my finished book.

Foreword by Ven. Lekshe

Books that translate the core teachings of the Buddha for non-Buddhists, as well as Buddhists, are precious. By including personal stories about the writer's and other women's experiences, this book is especially meaningful for women readers. Further, it is an invaluable read for men and anyone dissatisfied with their job or experiencing that uncomfortable feeling we all have when life isn't working. The feeling may be waking up to an inner conflict about our career or direction. It may be an intuitive sense that the path we are following conflicts with our inner life. It may be a gnawing awareness that "I'm not at home here even though I have worked hard to get here" or simply "Why don't I feel happy with my life?"

On the outside, everything may seem fine and going according to plan. On the other end of the spectrum, life may feel like a total disaster. In either case, we may rely on various distractions to avoid confronting an inner conflict that we may be unable to verbalize. Even if we put words to it, the conflict may seem unresolvable. Eventually, we may find that constantly grasping at one distraction after another is not working. Finally, we realize we're out of balance but don't know why.

Young people these days often grapple with an identity crisis like this. Many find that, although they are achieving the goals they set for themselves, they are uncomfortable with the person they have become. But, perhaps more critically, they wake up to the reality that, ultimately, only they can find a solution to their unease.

Some treat this inner crisis with drugs or therapy. These placebos may be of some benefit, but wise ones come to realize that success is tenuous and true happiness and contentment are elusive. Our emotions, intuitions, and dreams become stagnant or silent when life becomes entirely directed toward outward pursuits. As a result, our inner spirit becomes crushed. This book directly addresses that kind of spiritual crisis.

What's the solution to a spiritual crisis? Barua deftly identifies the causes and consequences, then proposes a resolution to the teachings of the Buddha. It was precisely a sense of spiritual crisis that distressed the Buddha, a young prince who had everything and thought he understood life. One day, he discovered that he was clueless about the human situation and sought to understand the sufferings rooted in his ignorance. This book is a contemporary interpretation of the wisdom that unfolded in his process of discovery.

Working through our suffering is necessarily based on our own human experience. Only after we work through various layers of repression and confusion do we realize that our feelings of unease stem from our heart-mind, and our spiritual life has been neglected. Barua translates this knowledge into language accessible to anyone facing a spiritual crisis. She systematizes the Buddha's teachings into guidelines that any individual can follow in their process of evolving self-knowledge. These teachings can be customized for each person's human expression. The inner desire to be happy and at peace with life comes to fruition and benefits all living beings.

Essentially, the teachings begin with an open mind of inquiry and simple reflections that are universal. These teachings are non-sectarian and non-religious. Barua calls them AWE, "Six A's for Awakening with Ease." The process begins with an inner investigation, recognizing old fear-based paradigms and conditioning by turning our attention inward. This self-discovery process is personal and experiential, undertaken with loving care. This internal inquiry steadily leads to deeper and deeper understanding. We proceed with the search at our own pace. The process is simple, and we can take as much time as we need. Wisdom flows freely as we progress at our own rate. This is not a test or a trial. It is a genuine path of self-discovery, unique to each of us.

Self-knowledge is an understanding of our internal process. Once we are ready, we begin the following steps: cultivating a kind heart, an open mind, and a wholesome mindset. The book guides us through the practices and insights that allow us to grow naturally into a whole new understanding of the human condition. This path leads to self-acceptance, inner peace, and acceptance of everyone else. Gradually, through mindful, spiritual practice and deep contemplation, we develop inner strength and bountiful love that transcends ourselves. Therein lies true liberation.

—Karma Lekshe Tsomo (Patricia Zenn), Buddhist Nun, Scholar, Author and Social Activist, Co-founder of Sakyadhita International Association of Buddhist Women and Founding Director of Jamyang Foundation

Introduction

*"Your own self-realization is the greatest service
you can render the world."*
-Ramana Maharshi

*"Educating the mind without educating the heart
is no education at all."*
-Aristotle

This book is about awakening from the conventional social myth of happiness and freedom based on competition, consumption, and accumulation to a deeper dimension of life that is aligned with our loving, wise, kind, and joyful nature, our true purpose, and a mindful noble life committed to personal and planetary evolution and awakening. The aim of this contemplative, meditative life is to go beyond the limits of one's gender, culture, religion, social roles, and identities that create otherness, unnecessary conflicts, suffering, and delusions to embrace our shared human experience, evolution, and journey to whole-hearted enlightenment. We have the capacity to access the unbounded realms of the infinite mind, universal intelligence, and living vision of a world based on enlightened presence, deliberate intent, right use of power, and wise action.

This book is written as a guide for a new paradigm: by focusing on what one loves and what brings one peace and joy. This guide is meant for modern-day seekers, especially brave women and minority groups of spiritual courage navigating through the maze of male and white institutional norms, expectations, biases, and internalized systems of oppression in society. It is also for the first-generation immigrants, conscious entrepreneurs, mindful leaders, and changemakers in an unconscious world, who are wanting to self-actualize, their own authentic nature going beyond self-doubt, fear, and ignorance to realize their vision of happiness and freedom beyond the egoic self. So they can use their true gifts in the service of people and planet in a fast-changing world.

Awakening, nirvana, or enlightenment is a doorway to the new planetary paradigm in human consciousness. It is a quantum shift registered in human conscious mind, often accompanied by inner illumination, oneness, ecstasy, entry to void, quantum zero-point field of infinite potential, emptiness, end of self-identity, sublime peace, total freedom, and absolute awe beyond all space-time-dimension conditioning. It is a life changing, metamorphic evolutionary potential that exists untapped in the inherent awareness and natural intelligence of the human heart-mind (*citta*).

This direct experience of awakening profoundly shifts one's view of reality, self, mind, and nature of life, existence, and cosmos irreversibly. The energetic impact of individual awakening can sometimes be felt as an echo and powerful vortex of energy in the human body. This higher dimensional pure energy of peace, unconditional love, and bliss can catalyze the social and collective awakening of many. There is nothing more powerful than the power of a well-cultivated quiet, still, and pure mind.

The *Oxford English Dictionary* describes awakening as 1) an act of waking up from sleep and 2) the act of suddenly becoming aware of something. In this book, awakening or enlightenment means awakening from a state of repeated suffering and the wheel of birth and death due to causes like:

1. Lack of awareness, unconscious ignorance, misperception, and wrong views about the true nature of reality, life, self, and mind

2. Habitual mental conditioning, disposition, and karmic patterns (*samkhara*) that keep us chained to craving, aversion, delusion, doubt, and fear, blame and shame, gain and loss of ordinary conventional life

Of all the things that make humans unique, needing purpose, meaning and a sense of liberation in our lives is one of the most prominent. The process of awakening I describe in this book is intended as support for modern day seekers and contemplatives, who find themselves without the privilege or support of a personal teacher, *sangha*, spiritual friend, family, or favorable environment.

Do you know the difference between conventional religion and unconventional spirituality? Religion is a specific set of organized and institutionalized beliefs and practices around one God or many gods, usually led by a hierarchy of institutionalized clergy or priests in a community or group. Spirituality is an individual's search for meaning, purpose, authentic self, service beyond ego, and direct connection with source, universal truth, or divine oneness with All that is, without external imposition of dogma, fixed beliefs, and rituals.

The Buddha was a great educator, observer, spiritual leader, and deep thinker of human nature and human suffering. His discovery of the path to awakening and liberation is called going against the stream of conventional truth, the stream of convention, and collective habits of bias, greed, hate, sectarianism, and selfishness to cultivate virtue and establish an open heart-mind of loving-awareness. He gave a systematic, complete, and coherent system of universal teachings for developing the human mind and personality. As we face multiple crises on the planet, including crises in leadership at the top, we need awakened leaders, CEOs, entrepreneurs, authors, and changemakers who can embody and model the way, inspire shared vision, and wise ethical action.

Awakening With Ease (AWE) is an awareness-based process for self-discovery, self-knowledge, contemplative inquiry, and meditation practices leading to stages of self-Awakening, also called enlightenment or *bodhi*. A loving heart and an open mind with a sense of wise adventure, fearless wonder, and compassionate curiosity to experience the unknown is all that is needed to put AWE into a daily practice of cultivation of awareness or mindfulness.

If you see yourself as a mindful leader, professional woman, unsupported immigrant, spirit-led entrepreneur, person of color, new paradigm maker, or disadvantaged and without privilege, yet share a deep heart-felt desire for wisdom and freedom from fear and ignorance, the root cause of all human sickness and suffering, and a love of inner peace, calm, happiness, universal knowledge, truth, understanding, and profound wisdom—this book is for you. I am happy you are reading this.

This book will help you shift your inner paradigm of scarcity, fear, greed, hate, and delusion to a paradigm of love, awareness, generosity, wisdom, and compassion. Awakening With Ease (AWE) means recognizing your inherent human capacity to know, observe, and be aware of your direct experience without reactivity now and remembering your own experiential journey with radical honesty, acceptance, loving awareness, and compassion.

The planetwide lockdowns and daily death statistics interrupted our routine autopilot life. It is as if a systemwide reset button has been pushed and now we are rebooting. Many of us are reflecting on our new priorities and new direction in life and many are leaving jobs and relationships beyond the wheel of survival fear, stress, and loneliness. The World Health Organization says the pandemic has sparked a 25 percent increase in anxiety and depression worldwide. Time magazine reports extreme poverty and inequality (people living below $1.90 a day) has risen by a quarter of a billion people (total 860 million) due to the impact of the COVID-19 in 2022.

In this time of multiple crises, humanity is poised for a great collective awakening and peaceful revolution in human consciousness. A collective awakening spurred by individual awakening across culture, gender, race, religion, and political divides can turn the tide in this time of greatest challenge to the greatest opportunity for humanity to heal generational trauma and transform and shift to sustainable solutions and right actions for the next seven generations and beyond.

Each of us is called to be an agent of change, leader, volunteer, guide, mentor, teacher, and someone who shows the way by being the change in our own relationship with ourselves and in our home, work, extended family, community, and country. We urgently need a spiritual science of regeneration, wise attention, fierce compassion, unsinkable hope, and endless possibilities to reimagine and recreate. Now is not the time for a fear-based science of doom and gloom and harmful technology that can kill the planet in a heartbeat. Strategic investment in education of self-awareness, conscious business, mindful self-leadership, and awakening of human consciousness must take priority at the highest level of the UN, national governments, and private corporations.

The New Earth Paradigm based on social awakening is already happening worldwide. Data from the 2020 Global Peace Index shows that civil unrest has doubled over the last decade. Between 2011 and 2018, the number of protests and riots roughly doubled, while the number of general strikes quadrupled, from 33 events in 2011 to 135 in 2018. Non-violent mass movements are increasing. Recent quantitative research has demonstrated that nonviolent strategies are twice as effective as violent ones. Organized and disciplined nonviolence can disarm and change the world, along with our lives, our relationships, and our communities.

Why awakening is important now

There is so much unnecessary pain, conflict, division, and confusion in our world. Even our "experts" are trapped into systems of oppression, dualism, polarized, or one-dimensional thinking. This book gives a simple roadmap to transform pain to self-healing, confusion to clarity, mental fog and doubt to awareness and wisdom, and restores your true nature and connection with All that is.

It all starts with a beginner's mind.

Beginner's mind is full of wonder, awe, and curiosity. Shun-ryu Suzuki (author of *Zen Mind, Beginner's Mind*) says, "In the beginner's mind, there are many possibilities, but in the expert's, there are few". With the beginner's mind, your mind will be unobstructed, open to change, and accepting of new ways of learning, seeing, and knowing. The awakening process is also connected with progressively integrating your life and true nature with your vision, intuition, and creativity. That's what Awakening With Ease (AWE) is all about.

That's where we want to begin. And that's where the magic happens.

I understand the kinds of complex challenges you're going through, whether you're a working woman, minority entrepreneur, a changemaker, a person of color, or first-generation immigrant. I went through challenges and barriers in both my professional work and spiritual practice in mostly white workplaces and *sanghas* (spiritual communities).

It's not easy.

Traditionally both women and ethnic minorities are accustomed to being ignored, trivialized, dismissed, and debased. A recent *Forbes* article names those barriers as minority stress in dominant culture as imposter syndrome, fear of missing out (FOMO), perfectionism, stereotype threat, inability to self-promote and step-up, fear of failure, judgment, loss of work, and fear of expressing vulnerability. In 2019, the proportion of women in senior management roles globally grew to 29%. According to the World Economic Forum's Global Gender Gap Report, it will still be 170 years until women achieve economic parity on a global scale. Yet shifts in consciousness can happen in a heart's beat.

Fast reverse 2,600 years ago, five years after the Buddha's enlightenment, to when his aunt and foster mother, Mahapajapati Gotami, was perhaps the first recorded humanist feminist who requested for *bhikkhuni* (nuns) ordination of herself and her five hundred female companions. The Buddha relented at first (perhaps the timing and other factors were not suitable at that time) but consented soon after. Even today, gender and color disparity is a longstanding problem in many Buddhist *sanghas* and institutions, despite of the recent *bhikkhuni* revival movement globally.

An identity crisis is a developmental event that involves a person questioning their sense of self or place in the world. It's not just women or minorities. This kind of spiritual dilemma is not uncommon and is experienced by both young and old adults, parents, teachers, managers, counselors, and mental health professionals. Awakening is the desire to break free of all limitations of narrow identity, story, and oppression, both socially conditioned and personally constructed. It cannot be understood by the intellect or conceptual mind. Developmental psychologist Erik Erikson believed that the formation of identity was one of the most important conflicts that people face.

In this book you'll discover

The value of our precious human birth and our human potential to spiritually grow and awaken to our enlightened nature by cultivating awareness and wise attention. Both ancient spirituality and basic science agree on the innate human capacity for spiritual awareness. Such awareness evolves the human brain beyond survival fear mode, reduces stress and reactivity, and enables integration of the whole brain, meta cognition, psychological resilience, love of life, compassion, and skillful behavior.

- Spiritual growth is the gradual process of opening the heart-mind and raising the vibration of conscious-awareness beyond the ordinary, everyday mundane egoic existence. Awakening to some universal truth and principles of life, existence, and reality is a total paradigm shift to supramundane awareness of infinite selfless self. There is no one (self) home in the void! It means going beyond the ordinary mind and the ego and realizing who you really are, your true nature, and your connection to the source, cosmic void, and superconscious divine intelligence. You have the capacity to bridge time, space, and dimension within the realms of form and formlessness in your consciousness through meditative focus and stillness.

- The big picture view of the Buddha and his significance, not only as a remarkable ancient educator, thought leader, influencer, and changemaker of humanity, but also his approach to reduce human suffering and ignorance through cultivation of heart-mind through the inner technology of awareness was second to none. His mindfulness methods, inquiry, and frameworks are still relevant, effective, and useful for personal leadership, mental-psychological development, and social awakening for the modern secular society today.

- Mindfulness has become more mainstream within progressive secular business organizations and leadership with the support of numerous scientific studies. It is used in the health and wellness, technology, and finance sectors; legal and non-profit organizations; and in public service, education, prison, police, and even the military.

- An introduction to the six steps to AWE (Awakening With Ease) to move from unwholesome to wholesome, stress reduction to stress transformation, and toward self-transcendence and ultimate liberation.

- A simple version of the vast teachings of the Buddha, adapted for modern times (without needing any religious dogma or ritual) in just six beginner-to-advanced steps. Dharma books, suttas, and discussions are abundant now in many online sites and forums. One can easily do further study and contemplation to refine practice, sustain mindfulness, and develop calm and insight.

- Inspiration and encouragement to know that the path to awakening given by the Buddha is still accessible and realizable to those who listen and follow with open heart-mind and right effort.

- This is your invitation to study and remember this path to direct knowledge and liberation and not forget it so we can collectively change the paradigm and systems of greed, fear, hate, and delusion from the inside with non-violence, wisdom, and compassion. This book is also a primer for my next book on mindful system change.

How to use this book and what to expect

What you will find in the following pages can be applied to multiple aspects in your life, such as daily mindful living, livelihood, career, health, well-being, relationships, leadership, success, happiness, peace, purpose, meaning, joy, liberation, and more. If you love stories more than processing information, go to Part II first to read my memoir in a few mustard seeds. Then the back cover and foreword. Take a small bite to reflect and contemplate.

This book offers simple steps that you can implement right now to transform pains to power and challenges to opportunities for growth. Read the table of contents and go to the section that grabs your attention. In this book, you will find the universal thinking, thought leadership, wisdom, and compassion needed for your personal, professional, and spiritual growth now. Here you will find a simple roadmap, and a sustainable process of establishing the six bases for Awakening With Ease (AWE). Plus, you will find more awareness and inspiration to catalyze your spiritual potential, purpose, influence, quiet impact, and awakened legacy in the world.

You are about to discover perspectives, strategies, awareness enhancing tools, and processes on discovering the purpose of your own life journey in relation to the evolution of the whole.

You can bring the beauty, joys and sorrows, and wisdom and strengths of your own wakeful experiences and mistakes as you reflect on what you read here. Perhaps you can keep a journal about it for your grandchildren. We all have to die sooner or later and cannot take anything to the other side—none of our dear relations, our precious belongings, not even our body that we so cherish. Making friends with death and dying is a deep, spiritual practice. The only thing we take is our wisdom and our karma.

This isn't like any other book you have read

It is saturated with direct experiences, reflections, quotes, phrases, and takeaways that can be applied by every person interested in cultivating an intelligent mind, higher consciousness, ultimate truth, knowledge, and wisdom, with or without prior knowledge of spirituality or Buddha *dharma*.

It is inspired by timeless teachings of Buddha and other wise beings and proven methods that have been used by professional women, single moms, immigrants, mindful business leaders, entrepreneurs, innovators, experts, artists, creators, underprivileged minorities, and contemplative students in the past and will continue in the future.

I have written this book as an unconventional narrative that is conversational with stories, imagery, anecdotes, provocative questions, action steps, case studies, and multiple opportunities for you to reflect, get clear, take notes, journal, and take action,

What I offer is a practical framework for being a wiser and kinder version of yourself, a more purposeful, mindfulness practitioner, and a better inquirer, meditator, communicator, and more influential leader in any field, whether awakening or ending suffering by ending ignorance is your immediate and urgent focus or not.

My intention is that you develop enough self-love, trust, and confidence in yourself and the regularity of *dhamma* that you are able to generate the quiet impact, influence, and happiness you want, which will impact your health, well-being, relationships, income, and the quality of life we all seek. You are about to discover a better way to do practice by alignment of energies of mind-body-emotion-spirit and the spiritual science of mindfulness with the pyramid of the six "A" steps to AWE (Awakening With Ease). These six steps can also be seen as six energetic keys to open the doorways to AWE to deeper levels.

- Alive
- Ask
- Abandon
- Accept
- Aware
- Awaken

A Quick Hello

I am Susmita aka Acharya Navasajiiva (*nava* means "new" and *sajiva* means "alive" or "endowed with new life"). This name was given to me in 2016 as an ordained Buddhist lay minister by my spiritual friends and guides Venerables Pannavati and Pannadipa of the Multilineage Contemplative Order of the Simplicity Hermitage.

I am also a certified professional coach, and worked as a city planner, housing and special projects coordinator, advisor, and consultant for small business and nonprofits and volunteer for many causes, including:

- Ambassador for the World March for Peace
- President and advocate for the Alliance for Bhikkhunis
- Women's prison
- Local hospice
- Developer of the Buddhist Women's Network on LinkedIn
- The New Economic Paradigm, Buddhist Facebook page
- Blogs on Women, Evolution, Enlightenment, TreenaNeel, and Deep Conscious Capitalism.
- Founding Member KY Meditation Peace Center, Sakyadhita USA, Heartwood Refuge, Foundation of Women's Education in Rural World, and Life Member of the Dharmankur, Bengal Buddhist Association.

I also completed two master's degrees, one from the University of Calcutta and one from the University of Arizona in geography and planning.

Having been born in a minority Bengali Barua Buddhist family in India, I was organically exposed and inspired by Buddha and his teachings from my sporadic study, inquiry, early dreams, intuitions, and travels to Buddhist pilgrimage sites. I started teaching my own understanding of spirituality and dhamma without any credentials in 2004 in public libraries and taught my first women's retreat on the "Primordial Path to Natural Awakening" at the Zen Furnace Mountain, KY, in 2007. I also initiated and co-led a day retreat on the "Wisdom of the Feminine Principle" at the Lexington Shambhala center.

My intention is to make it easy for people to integrate *dhamma* in their daily life, business, relationship, and social network engagements in an organic way, connecting with what is alive in them and what brings them joy, healing, health, wisdom, and happiness. Wisdom is the source of wise wealth, spiritual friendship, and happiness.

Some of my happy moments as a public speaker happened by synchronicities in international and national forums like Sakyadhita (four times), IABU (International Association of Buddhist Universities), US Basic Income Group, National Council of Independent Scholars, US Social Forum II, World March for Peace, and many others.

This book is a natural support and guide for modern day seekers and contemplatives who often find them as misfits in their professional work, as their vision, way of thinking and ideas do not fit the conventional form, and who are committed to put into action the spiritual practice and process of

Awakening With Ease (AWE) with clarity, confidence, and courage.

Although it is written in first person from the perspective of an immigrant Indian Buddhist woman of Bengali origin, it is presented in a modern format. You will find many parallels from the early Buddhist map of the process of awakening.

And even if you don't know anything about the Buddha, you will love this!

The AWE method: how and why it works

The intention behind this book is to bring wise attention to our individual and collective ignorance (unconsciousness) and give a simple six "A" stages roadmap to end the ignorance about life and human existence that is causing so much pain, disconnection, oppression, injustice, and suffering in the world. The six combination keys to the AWE transformation process are:

more (Aliveness)+ This step connects us with our physical body and senses, natural breathing, vital energetic body and the easy rhythm of our heart. Tuning into our heart and physical senses resets our energy, attention, and awareness from habitual unconscious and autopilot mode to conscious and deliberate mode. Recognizing what makes us alert, alive, and happy now also reconnects and rebalances the vital energy within us with the greater life force in nature. It connects us with present moment experience and choices, and problems slowly fall away. Problems exist in the past and future.

more (Asking)+ This step can also be called right inquiry or investigation of life, nature of reality, and *dhamma* (universal truth). Asking the right question in the right or skillful way leads us to the right view, right understanding, right knowledge, direction, and destination (end of ignorance and suffering). Sustained mindful inquiry on any subject requires an open mind, good intention, safe space, deep listening, and compassion.

more (Abandoning)+ We slowly release our attention and energy from anything unwholesome (in body, mind, and speech habits) that depletes our energy and repels others to a more wholesome state of mind of contentment without habitual lack and fear. Cultivating wise and caring habits toward self and others gives us courage and confidence to go forward, even in the face of pain and fear.

more (Acceptance)+ Here we become open as a humble student and observer of life and nature. We gradually release control, resistance, and reactivity to external people or situations as we feel more spacious, resourceful, and alive from the inside out. We begin to see that we can consciously choose our boundary and response before, during, and after an event based on our own principles in a caring way that frees us from all kinds of limiting beliefs, control, and powerlessness. Our trauma heals, relationships transform, our mood uplifts, and our impact endures.

more (Awareness)+ Awareness brings light and love to all areas hidden from our conscious-awareness. Establishing awareness in the four domains of human experience—breath-body, contact-feeling, heart-mind state, nature of reality-mind-self (*dharma*)—is the way to remove ignorance and develop insight into human suffering. It was the compassionate way and direct path discovered by the Buddha to liberate humanity from ignorance, doubt, identity view, craving, and suffering.

more (Awakening)+ Here, mind is consistently inclined and devoted to the great heart-mind of awakening (*bodhicitta*) through progressive unification and alignment of mindfulness, inquiry, energy of courage, joyful effort, calm-serenity, still focus, and great unshakable equanimity. One generates perception of light and a luminous mind by meditating on the sun and full moon. One does not cling to any mental state or signs (*nimitta*), no matter how blissful.

My short story

What can an individual do in a dysfunctional, white male environment, when the whole planet seems to be headed the wrong way? This is the question that loomed large in my consciousness as I resigned from my professional job as city planner at age thirty-three. I felt I had come to a crossroads and a dead-end with no clear path forward. I could not go on living with business as usual. I took the road less traveled to know what color my parachute was. I decided to stop, take a long uncertain pause, and put all my attention on my own self-care and care of our four-year-old daughter. This was not easy after two graduate degrees (one in India) and a lot of hard work in a land and culture far from home. I took refuge in my sad, breathing heart to stop my overthinking, anxious mind.

1. Recollected important early life events, sensory memories, travels, dreams, influences, and achievements
2. Asked deep questions, which activated the inner GPS of the wise heart. It remembers and knows more than you think you know.
3. Tuned into the wonder, curiosity, and playfulness of the inner magical child by being fully present with my four-year-old daughter
4. Aroused urgency about ending ignorance and suffering
5. Developed clear awareness of wholesome and unwholesome, applying right effort
6. Singularly focused and resolved from the beginning to end ignorance and to find ultimate knowledge and liberation

What I attempt to share here is a way to irreversible happiness and freedom that can be described as ending suffering by ending ignorance.

The myths of spiritual awakening

Myths are unexamined belief systems, legends, views coming from religion, culture, society, history, groups, legends, secular institutions, media, and even conservative science. Myths influence our culture and shape our perception of who we are and how we treat others, ourselves, and our planet. They can become limiting beliefs, doubts, and wrong views about what we can and cannot do in this world or next. With awareness, we let them go and affirm positive statements and goodwill toward all.

The human brain creates reality from its subconscious belief system or programming. Science now tells us that the early childhood experiences of people deeply affect their future physical, cognitive, emotional, and social development. With mindful-awareness meditation, all the harmful tendencies and habits of body, mind, and speech (*akusala sankhara*, in the words of the Buddha) can be recognized, changed, and rewritten for our human brain to function optimally. Awakening not only leads to irreversible and permanent shifts in mindset and level of awareness but also deepens our direct knowledge, profound wisdom, and compassion for all beings.

Most people do not explore their inner life because there are many myths and confusion about the meaning of spirituality, enlightenment, and awakening.

- It is hard and only for monks. This was not true even in Buddha's time, People from all different backgrounds including householder, king, queen, farmer, trader, women, servant, senior, young, and old all experienced various stages of awakening. Some suttas mention one becomes a monk after *arahantship*, the last and final stage of awakening. There is much a lay person can do to take the first step and advance on the path.

- I'm not religious. Actually Buddha's teachings are very suitable for secular society without any dogma or belief in soul, Creator God, and rituals. The teachings are mostly education for developing a calm, non-reactive and ethical heart-mind with the aim of growing in wisdom and compassion and ending suffering by ending greed, hate, and ignorance. The emphasis is on discovering truth for oneself through one's own effort and taking responsibility for one's own intentional action and choices. Embracing all beings and life now, with its constantly changing, co-dependent, and self-less impersonal nature moment to moment, is a deep practice of mindfulness.

- What's the point? The point is to end human suffering by ending ignorance. The teachings can transform the quality and happiness in any stage and all areas of life. Ignorance is not bliss. Wisdom is bliss. Ignorance of the nature of reality (impermanence, interdependence, not-self) is the greatest cause of disconnection, pain, and suffering (*dukkha*) on the planet.

- Have no time for meditation. Developing any new habit takes time, patience, psychological safety, and practice. Studies have shown introducing micro-habits—like taking a minute or two pause for mindful breathing or simply connecting to loving warm feelings in the heart—can interrupt stressful habits of over-thinking, judgment, anger, resentment, blame, and anxiety patterns in many. Start with five minutes of slow breathing meditation before sleep or after waking. There are many opportunities throughout the day to take a pause and be present and mindful.

- Do not want to vanish. *Nirvana* is often described as extinguishment (of the fire of greed, hate and delusion) in the suttas. This along with the idea of not-self (*anatta*) create a fear for some novice and even advanced practitioners. Buddha or any of his *arahants* did not vanish from this reality after awakening. Buddha took the responsibility to teach for forty-five years after his enlightenment, until his physical death, out of compassion for the welfare and benefit of all beings. I heard of a few people (including myself) who had vivid visions of Buddha in either awake or lucid dream state. Who knows, Buddha may be still teaching in the inner planes!

- Individual awakening is a selfish thing. How does it help the world? Awakening is breaking through the egoic structures and identity view (*sakkaya ditthi*), which keeps the old delusional habits of racism, sexism, extreme nationalism, capitalism, identity-politics, and all kinds of divisiveness, schisms, war, and conflict in society and between nations in place. Awakening simply reconnects an individual with the Universal energies of the fifth and higher dimension of consciousness so we thrive from our true selfless nature. Is breaking through a cocoon to become a butterfly selfish?

- Peace is impossible! People take voluntary refuge in Buddha (awakened one), *dhamma* (his teachings), and *sangha* (wise community of practitioners) to practice generosity, ethics, meditation, and wisdom. These practices help create the true and unshakable foundation for peace, happiness, wise conduct, and compassionate action to address challenges that threaten peace, both at home and the world. Once, I wrote a sign in an anti-war rally, "In the power of peace, all fear and terror cease." Peace is possible from inside out when we begin to practice mindful-awareness daily and the sense of separate ego-self dissolves.

- A woman cannot be enlightened. This myth is strong in many parts of the world and is based on ignorance. As long as a woman, man, or third gender is identified with physical body or any personal-social-sexual identity, they cannot go beyond the conventional to the non-physical supramundane reality of *ariya* or noble ones, who reach it through wisdom, generosity, ethics, and mindful-meditation (*samma sati* and *samma samadhi*).

  The Buddha acknowledged thirteen enlightened Arhat nuns for their foremost qualities, including his own stepmother, his aunt Mahapajapati, and his wife Yashodhara. Therigatha is a record of the earliest spiritual women's literature with many short poems spoken by or about enlightened nuns (*theris*). Khujjuttarā, a servant of Queen Samavati, was recognized by Buddha as being the foremost lay and learned female disciple of Buddha, for teaching as many as five hundred women to become awakened as stream-enterers.

The Buddha gave specific antidotes and the tools for mindful living for going against the stream of greed, hate, and delusional self that we see in the leaders at home and the world today. Peaceful paradigm shifts happen when people recognize wisdom and compassion within them and choose to follow their inner guidance and the wise leaders who embody *dhamma* (over corrupt ones), irrespective of gender, race, class, caste, religion, and other social or political identities.

Connect and schedule a call now at my website (susmitabarua.com), LinkedIn (linkedin.com/in/susmitabarua), or Facebook (facebook.com/mindfulgeniusu) for any guidance, coaching, or ongoing support you may need to put the six "A" steps to practice. This book is meant to simplify your practice and go deeper than you ever have before.

Please research the Buddhist terms and Pali suttas mentioned here (see site references at the end of book). Make a plan, such as studying one chapter or section and suttas mentioned for a week or two. Log your daily minutes of contemplation and meditation to establish beneficial micro-habits. Write your intention for study and practice. Develop and follow a consistent practice schedule (not too tight, not too loose) no matter how small.

Part I

"Come, Kalamas. Do not go upon what has been acquired by repeated hearing, nor upon tradition, nor upon rumor, nor upon scripture, nor upon surmise, nor upon axiom, nor upon specious reasoning, nor upon bias toward a notion pondered over, nor upon another's seeming ability, nor upon the consideration 'The monk is our teacher.' When you yourselves know: 'These things are bad, blamable, censured by the wise; undertaken and observed, these things lead to harm and ill,' abandon them... When you yourselves know: 'These things are good, blameless, praised by the wise; undertaken and observed, these things lead to benefit and happiness,' enter on and abide in them."

-The Buddha on Free Inquiry, Kalama Sutta AN 3:65

CHAPTER 1

My Memoir in a Few Mustard Seeds

"Thousands of candles can be lighted from a single candle, and the life of the candle will not be shortened. Happiness never decreases by being shared."
-Buddha

"It is through gratitude for the present moment that the spiritual dimension of life opens up."
-Eckhart Tolle

On a bright summer day, a little four-year-old girl was playing hide-and-seek with her playmates in a Calcutta neighborhood street. It was lined by two-story yellow brick housing built for government civil servants. With the sound of a whistle (sounds better), everyone ran in five directions, leaving the little girl alone to do the seeking. She looked up at the sun for help. Suddenly, she became aware of an all-pervading awareness that was empty, open, vast, and sky-like.

That little girl was me. I just had a glimpse of a vast empty awareness of what I might call the original mind. I felt ecstatic joy and asked my open awareness (imaginary friend) why this game of hide-and-seek was so exciting. I heard a silent voice clearly in my inner ear: "Because you know without a doubt nobody is lost forever (in space-time). You know you will eventually find your friends and each other."

There was an instant recognition within me that this big mind or open awareness knew much more than this little child's body-mind playing on the neighborhood street. This was my first experience of my inner self providing instruction about the nature of mind. I felt that I could trust this silent voice and unseen presence. A trusting relationship with this aware inner voice developed naturally in subsequent years.

I had a similar joyful and expansive awareness with heightened inner sense perceptions while visiting the ocean for the first time with family and while visiting many Buddhist sites during our family travels from ages nine to nineteen. While climbing up the steps to Vulture Peak at Rajgir was quite hard with my grandma, I kept going. I held my widowed grandma's hands, who also had arthritic knees, and kept saying, "Granny, my tummy hurts!" In contrast I had a joyful descent down the steps after seeing the places where Buddha sat, taught, and stayed many times with his disciples. I wondered why the descent felt so easy and joyful? I recall the strong inner urge I felt to take a leap off the cliff of the Vulture Peak and fly like a bird.

One day, my father took me aside and told me about not forgetting our vanishing Barua Buddhist clan who survived in the coastal area of Chittagong, Bangladesh (which was part of undivided India before 1945), as *Buddhadharma* disappeared from the plains of India. I listened and interpreted that as my father indirectly asking me to marry within the clan. In my ancestry, I had a great-grandfather and Buddhist monk by the name of Ven. Kripasaran Mahasthavir (1865-1926), who did pioneer work in the Buddhist revival movement in India along with Anagarika Dharmapala of Sri Lanka and established many viharas in different cities. My first training on mindfulness was on mindful eating and other chores. That came from my grandma. She was a close, sister-like friend and relative of the late Dipama, the Buddhist meditation master, and founding mother of the *vipassana* community in the US. I have a few fond memories of meeting her and Dipa a few times in our home and hers.

I had vivid memories of pre-school childhood events when I was fully aware with clear comprehension of what was happening in my home or classroom environment in teacher-student or parent-child interactions. A few unpleasant experiences at home and school dropped away more easily from my conscious mind, but positive ones stayed much longer as I would often remember and reflect on them.

One of my earliest dream memories was falling like a feather in a spiraling motion and waking up on the bed as a little child on this plane. My immediate first thought was, *Have I sinned?* The next thought was, *I am a Buddhist in this life, not a Christian.* At that very young age (three or four years old) I did not consciously know anything about my religious identity. This was perhaps my first glimpse of a past-life memory and inquiry.

When I was in third grade, our family of six moved to a separate private house from the apartment complex with multi-language residents from different states of India. I was relocated to a bigger public school away from the loving space of a tiny one-room home school downstairs with close friends and a very caring Anglo-Indian teaching couple. I had very fond memories of this home school and my first teachers.

By contrast, this new school (with a co-ed elementary and an all-girls middle and high school in the same large three-story school building) had somewhat punitive and angry elementary teachers. Here, I was subjected to public shaming three times in three years for careless, minor infractions. One infraction was simply sitting on a teacher's chair in an empty classroom. Role playing was not allowed and punished as disobedience. This impacted and regressed my curiosity and performance as a student from grades three to six and probably adversely impacted my voice as a teen and adult with adults and new people and situations for years.

However, one observant science teacher's wise attention and public appreciation of me in the classroom after a midterm exam turned around the situation for me in grade seven. I graduated summa cum laude from my school's secondary board exam to my own surprise and everyone else's. Two years later, my sister repeated the same streak with a higher overall score despite tremendous health challenges. This made our father, who was an accomplished student himself, very happy. I still remember my father's rare and genuine hug.

Q: What are the happiest memories of your time with yourself, family, and friends that you remember in your body?

- Around age ten, I had a significant lucid dream of the celestial Buddha in standing position with his five sitting disciples all in golden light bodies with white light robes. Strangely, I was witnessing them as a child from inside the hollow earth. This dream made me feel very safe and blessed. I spontaneously started chanting the Buddhist three jewel names—Buddha, *dharma*, and *sangha*—while falling asleep with a peaceful mind. I also wondered why it made me feel so calm, safe, and serene.

Q: Do you recall moments of serenity, peace, joy, and open awareness when you were quite young? Did any early dreams or sensory impressions imprint on you?

- From an invisible neighborhood school, I was accepted into an elite women's college in Calcutta named Lady Brabourne College. Our geography team of twelve girls stayed together like a very close-knit sisterhood for almost seven years. Most of us received National Merit Scholarships as undergraduates and graduated with master's degrees from the University of Calcutta in 1985. We are still in touch as spiritual friends via WhatsApp. I greatly missed this type of soul friendship after coming to the US.

Q: Can you recall the impact of some of your friends and teachers on you?

- Going to the college was fun despite the hour-long, hot, and sweaty commute in the hot, humid weather and the smelly, overcrowded public buses in Calcutta. Observing the sheer material poverty, extensive slums, and daily grind of huge masses of people in the streets of Calcutta had a huge impact on my psyche that never left me. My elective subjects of economics and political science left me more confused than before I started. I often wondered why humans create systems so entangled we do not comprehend them. I could sense my school imparted knowledge that was far removed from the reality of daily stress and grind of the common people everywhere.

Q: If you could change one thing or system on the planet what would that be?

- Soon, I had to leave my mom, family, and close-knit group of friends to pursue my dream of a life of adventure and learning in the US as a graduate student at the University of Arizona in Tucson. Adapting to many changes in weather, culture, food, language, lack of friends, and community was challenging. In the new land, I had difficulty forging the same kind of psychological safety, intimacy, and trust (as in Calcutta) with other students and people around me, even though I was friendly by nature.

- Fast forward ten years and at age thirty-three, I resigned from my profession as a socio-economic planner for the city. My life took an unexpected dip and detour. All my education and knowledge did not teach me the life skills needed to navigate complex changes in the work-life environment. Balancing two very different cultural expectations and navigating new relationships with my new family after marriage was not easy. Raising a colicky child after a C-section without any close family or friends around in a foreign land was the most challenging task I ever had. Plus, working full-time in a new job in a mostly white, all-male, and biased environment was emotionally exhausting and isolating. I had little clue why because my mind became emotionally agitated and rebellious from inside.

Q: Do you recall feeling lonely, emotionally overwhelmed, or triggered by multiple unexpected changes in a new and unfamiliar environment?

- My faith in conventional education as a way to create a thriving right livelihood and be happy hit rock bottom after my first job. I was determined that no job or person would control my destiny, time, attention, energy, health, and peace of mind. I knew if I did not regain my inner balance, my whole family would be imbalanced. The thought, *Ignorance is the cause of deepest suffering*, kept running through my mind. I also felt my pain was not separate from the collective pain and systemic oppression everyone felt, especially new moms and women of color, immigrants, and other minorities in any system of inequality, unconscious privilege, bias, hate, and unequal power.

Q: Have you ever felt unsupported and oppressed in your own home, school, work, or community from people close to you?

- I remembered the childhood epiphany I had after reading *The Children's Book of Knowledge*. Who should I take as my role model in education and knowledge? Would it be Einstein and mainstream materialistic science and technology of the five sensory world or the Buddha's inward-looking path of the sixth sense (heart-mind) that transcended the material world? I was inclined in favor of the Buddha (with his inner smile, insight, compassion, and happiness) over Einstein, where secular education was heading toward.

Buddha's invitation to "Come and see for yourself" (*ehipassiko*), to engage in free inquiry (Kalama Sutta) and encouragement for self-reliance and responsibility (be a refuge unto yourself) appealed to me. Because learning and knowledge is my passion, I held both sides lightly in my mind. Both are needed to live a wholesome life.

Q: What teachings or quote of Buddha appeals to your heart the most?

- Within five months of my resignation, my spouse lost his corporate management job, suddenly and unceremoniously. He was told to vacate the office in two hours with security guards present. He struggled more than me with his sudden job loss, as if he had lost his identity and self-worth. He had $20 in his pocket when he landed in the US to do his graduate studies leading to a PhD. Seven and a half years later, in 1993, our American dream life came tumbling down. It hit him hard. Surprisingly, I was undisturbed and calm due to my inner-guided mindfulness practice. I knew things would be okay. I gave him physical and emotional support to start his consulting business, which took more than three years to become sustainable. We lost our family health insurance (the most dreaded thing) until I found a second job. Recollection of three refuges, generosity of my parents, my own virtue, pilgrimage places, and my early dream of celestial Buddha all helped me stay steady through many rough patches in life.

The most important things in the book

Bring an open mind, wonder, curiosity, and inquiry as you read this book. The reason stories are meaningful is because they take you out of the linear, logical, and conceptual mindset to a more direct experiential and reflective mindset, which is the goal of the dharma life. Take one or a few simple reflection, inquiry and action strategies that appeal to you from this book. Reflect on your own journey; journal stories, questions, early influences that shaped your views. Become a sincere student of life. Human birth is precious, and we must learn not to waste it. Memorize the six "A" steps and work intentionally on one step at a time for the best samadhi or immersion experience.

Buddha's teachings are vast, and more available online now than ever before. Awakening With Ease (AWE) teachings are adapted and delivered in a modern, secular language (while retaining some key phrases and words from Pali). My intention is to offer this book for the liberation of many in a universal non-sectarian way, not just for Buddhists. I do not strictly identify with any particular Buddhist tradition, sangha, or lineage as my own experience without a teacher or scripture do not fit one tradition. The early pre-sectarian Buddhism appeals to me for its simplicity, precision, coherence, directness, humanism, and absence of religious dogma.

Modern-day practitioners coming from different cultural, religious, historical, linguistic, psychological backgrounds and scientific materialist outlook of a separate independent self with overlapping intersectional social identities and conflicting roles (which I experienced myself in my mostly white US graduate school, job, and sangha as a minority immigrant), along with the modern presence of greater self-doubt, irreverence, mistrust, addictive impulses and self-hatred among the converts, perhaps need a new and different approach.

Since I speak from my direct experience and embodied knowing, my hope is many will get the clarity, healing, wisdom, and clear comprehension necessary to realize the path in modern times. Trust your own intuition and direct experience and your own experiential journey than other people's opinion about you or the *Buddhadharma*.

My engaged spiritual work involved mostly peace and economic justice work with local, national, and international groups. I built my first spiritual website with a vision for the planet in three days following an inner urgency, eight months before 9-11 happened in 2001. I enjoyed work with local hospice and women's prison (about nine months each), workshops and retreats for women locally and with Sakyadhita International Buddhist Women's Conferences. In these conferences, I learned about the lack of support for Buddhist women and Theravada nuns and leadership opportunities for people of color in the mostly white sangha spaces. My Buddhist economics and mindful system change (since 2004) blogs, articles, podcasts, and speaking engagements were spontaneous experiments that arose from synchronicities of events, causes, and conditions.

This book is my urgent nudge for you to make your own spiritual growth, journey, and Awakening a priority in your life and to "Be a lamp and refuge unto yourself." I took these last departing words of the Buddha to his followers (Mahaparinibbana Sutta DN 16) to heart. I first read that quote as a child in a Mahabodhi Society Magazine. This book is about making the highest and best use of your precious human birth with the wholesome *bodhicitta* intention to live mindfully each day so you are ready to step whole-heartedly into the path of Awakening With Ease (AWE) for the benefit of all beings and the planet.

More on Awakening (AWE)

Awakening is both a gradual drop by drop incremental transformation process and a sudden quantum shift and breakthrough in Awareness. The discrete particle like entity (identity) crosses a threshold and realizes instantly, it is one with the unbounded, unconditioned, unified Source field. Awakening is both transcendental and immanent. All polarities, binary thinking and concepts collapse here in the ultimate reality of void (sunnya). Awareness is infused by a supramundane feeling tone of sublime peace, divine ecstasy, silent illumination and complete liberation of the individual personality from the conditioned reality of mind consciousness. All words, concepts and language fail here.

"It is this unshakable deliverance of heart-mind, that is the goal of this holy life, its heartwood and its end."
-Buddha (MN 29)

Awakening is both the highest and deepest peak experience of great intensity and transcendental depth that permanently shifts one's perception of reality, worldview, and self-view, yet restores trust and faith in life, human journey, and existence. Mind irreversibly shifts from all pervasive dissatisfaction, subconscious gossip, conflict, war, cynicism, pride, anxiety and negativity to unshakable inner peace, purity of perception, profound wisdom, love of all beings, joyful optimism, and compassionate action for the well-being of many.

AWE is an organic and natural approach to spiritual awakening and self-liberation from all mental-emotional pain, unwise habits, and suffering arising due to our culturally conditioned mind habits and socially constructed identity or self-view. These psycho-social habits are very deep rooted from ancestral-cultural-institutional lines as well as beginningless time. Reflecting on impermanence and non-self helps us release negative experiences and let go of wounding and hurtful things sooner than later.

Awakening is the outcome of learning wise habits of mind by removing the distorted filters and pollution of mind via greed, hate, and ignorance. Lack of education and awareness creates our limited and separate identity view of self and a fixed mindset around culture, gender, color, caste, religion, group identities, and divisive views. Our mind is conditioned by mental constructs of conceptual reality that is far removed from the true reality of things as they are.

I share a few critical elements, anecdotes, teachings, and case studies from my own journey and client experiences that you may find useful to boost your mindfulness practice to a state of flow, wonder, and ease. See your greatest challenge as a hidden opportunity for transformation and peak experience. Imagine how your life and the life of all you touch can change and shift if you take the Buddha's invitation (*ehipassiko - come and see for yourself*) as an experiment.

That is just what I did.

AWE involves connecting with one's heart's deepest intention and values, desire for well-being, need for healing, and using our inherent awareness and strengths to turn toward our pain when all our external support seemingly falls away.

By remaining a sincere student and observer of life, by remembering one's own wakeful, alive, inspired, and joyful experiences of clear seeing and knowing, and by recollecting those early role models who inspired our thinking and behavior, one can begin one's deliberate journey to awakening.

With development of awareness, one can discover one's unique path to one's own freedom, inner peace, joy, life purpose, and enlightened happiness.

The great turning inward

We have been trying too long to fix the world externally and get people and institutions to behave by force or legal punishment, and we all know how difficult it is to change a person's attitude, values, and conditioned mindset. Finding the courage to stop and turn inward toward our own pain, broken hearts, and mess ups is not so hard or unpleasant as our mind (inner critic) may tell us. Our willingness to extend the same kindness to ourselves as we would to our best friend when she is in trouble can help us survive the storm we are going through and turn the corner.

Stopping in the tracks of our unreflecting auto-pilot busy lives for some solitude, vision-questing, and self-care takes willingness, vulnerability, and courage. In the space of non-doing, deep-inquiry, and inner listening, we can retrieve our power of intuition, gut feeling, inner knowing, inherent wisdom, inspiration, compassion, and creative spark to retrieve our inner GPS to the heart's path, true nature, mindful vocation, and our mission in this life.

The prospect of having to quit my first professional job after two graduate degrees was painful. As a first-generation immigrant from India, I had made many sacrifices and hard adjustments to get to this point. It felt like a ton of bricks over my head and heart. The thought of leaving home and only child for a spiritual retreat or Ashram did not occur to me at all. Changing others was not an option or a possibility. So I quietly resigned and quit my career and the comfort of a regular paycheck. I renounced all future ambition as a professional planner for an uncertain unknown future. Looking back, that was the best decision I made in favor of my daughter, my family's future, and my own liberation and happiness.

Beginner's mind

My top priority then was to raise my only daughter mindfully without any rush or pressure of full-time work in a patriarchal environment. Taking better care of myself allowed me to be present with Maya, who was close to four years old then. During our brief time together at noon from her pre-school to babysitter's place, she often would beg me with her big imploring eyes, "Mommy, please stay five minutes more!" I felt guilty for leaving the office early to transport her from her preschool to the babysitter and also not being able to spend the extra five minutes with her so I could return to the office in time.

As a mother of an only child (I did not want another after the experience of the first one and seeing things as they are), I longed to spend my precious time, attention, and energy with Maya. By connecting with the beginner's mind and basic goodness (terms I knew and understood in my inner perception long ago without reading them), I started remembering wakeful moments in my own childhood. From observing Maya's development process, I am convinced that parenting is a great way to connect with our forever young spirit and playful wise inner child. Life is giving us a second chance to connect with our basic goodness and intrinsic happiness.

Mothers, especially from various minority and immigrant groups without extended family support are not doing well in America. They are underpaid and overworked and carry a huge mental and physical load. The US ranks fiftieth in the world in maternal mortality.

I became my own refuge and friend through the practice of what I call "unfabricated mindfulness" (seeing things as they are without story and filters as much as possible) and metta or loving-kindness, as both spontaneously arose in my mindstream. I reflected on my previous challenges as a student in three to four schooling environments and how I overcame them by being curious and inquisitive. These challenges actually offered me opportunities to be creative and to excel in my school exams.

Spiritual urgency of *samvega*

Bringing this sense of wonder, curiosity, and friendliness to my intense emotions of anger, fear, agitation, restlessness, resentments led me to see things as they are. These discursive thoughts and emotions were actually arising from conflicts with my various intersectional identity roles adopted in India and then in the US. My seven years of life as an immigrant woman gradually pulled me inward in a matter of weeks. As I listened deeply through my outer mental chatter, to factual reality without judgement, then paid attention to my complex feelings, and finally, context—meaning and identity a feeling of empathy, metta, and compassion naturally arose within me. And I was also raising our child with all the love a mother has for her only child. My shock and spiritual urgency to find a way out of suffering and ignorance unfolded like a choice between life and death for me. Only this time to a greater depth than ever before.

As a contemplative, I was somewhat clueless where all these deep emotions and distress signals were coming from. As if instead of the regular seven keys I am familiar with in my mind's keyboard, now thirty-six keys were playing on their own, pulling all my heart-mind and nerve strings. Many years later, I learned that I fit the description of an empath and HSP (highly sensitive person). I had no concept of internal boundaries and was absorbing a lot of painful energy from my environment.

My intention to find a way out helped me get very focused and singular with utmost relaxation that happens when mind naturally rests on spacious open awareness (non-conceptual mind). Fortunately, I regained my sanity and inner peace through an intense yet relaxed and calm introspective time of mindful-awareness and clear seeing, which started with right (wholesome) view and right (wholesome) intention for ending ignorance with right knowledge.

At the time, I was not consciously aware I was doing a Buddhist practice. I never had a formal teacher, sutta study, or even a meditation practice, yet I did go through an inner-guided awakening process of letting go, establishing mindfulness of breath-body, feeling, mental state, and a handful of *dhammas*, which was accompanied by seven factors of awakening.

What this means for you: You don't have to know everything. My wish here is to inspire many to listen to their inner voice and guidance during spiritual urgency (*samvega* need to be recognized in modern psychology). Trust your instinct, take *ehi-passiko* sincerely, and have faith in the Buddha and your own practice and process to Awakening. The energies in the planet now are such that many will awaken on their own if they are open minded and receptive. This inner paradigm shift in consciousness helps the evolution and ascension of the planet more than any external change in policies or regime.

Breakdown to breakthrough

In my child and teen years, I felt much joy, wonder, and awe in Buddha's discovery of a path to liberation to end human suffering, his open invitation to come and see (*ehipassiko*), the truth of his teachings for yourself, his affirmation to trust one's own direct experience, and paying attention to the words of wisdom of wise teachers. There was also his permission to the Kalama people to inquire and question the ultimate authority of all external sources of knowledge, including one's own teacher (Kalama Sutta AN 3.65) and his assurance to "be a lamp and refuge" to oneself by practicing true *dhamma*. I had a simple trust and faith in Buddha's words, much like a child has for her wise loving parents. The Kalama Sutta sets forth the principles that could be followed by a seeker of truth even today. I was immediately impressed by the Buddha's assertion to question and investigate all authoritative sources of information, including one's own teacher and Buddha himself.

The process I describe here was inspired by a handful teachings of the Buddha, and my own childhood and teen experiences. I had no teacher, no scripture, no spiritual friend at the time of great internal agitation and stress when *dhamma* pulled me inward. We all reside within *dharma*, the universal law of life and existence; just with a beginner's mind, clear awareness of wakeful moments in my life, and a strong intention to turn away from the forceful pull of the conventions in modern materialistic culture, its model of intellectual education (marginalizing cultivation of heart-mind and inner human experience), emphasizing external validation, job, status, and money as the measure of self-worth, happiness, and success is how I got started.

At the lowest point of my disillusionment with the treadmill of "auto-pilot life," I found the wholesome courage and energy (*viriya*) to quit my toxic job. By not abandoning my own internal needs, I faced my mental-emotional pain (*samvega*) and survival fear by taking refuge in my own awareness and my limitless love for my child and family. After a deliberate seven-month practice of contemplation, inquiry, and mindful-meditation, I had a profound superconscious awakening that completely changed my paradigm and previous worldview, my view of humanity, and the long-term trajectory of my life.

Recollection of past grief and joy

All my unexpressed and suppressed emotions from the past seven years since my arrival in the US surfaced in my recollections. Both at my job and in my new family and friends, I met a lot of unhappy, stressed out, judgmental, and disengaged people. Before this, I had seen my own father in India getting progressively sick with emphysema for seven years. He was gasping for his last breath before dying at only age fifty-eight, within seven months of his early retirement as an IRS officer for the government of India. Observing him, I became acutely aware of the importance of breath in being alive. I appreciated his wisdom and foresight in handing all family financial and real property details to meet our essential needs after his time on earth.

"Dear householder! That's the way it is—for sorrow,
lamentation, pain, distress, and despair
are born from one who is dear,
come springing from one who is dear."
–Buddha, Piyajatika sutta MN87

Life as an immigrant in the US

Strangely, by some karmic pull or psychic vision, I knew the person I was going to marry almost nine years before I met him in person. He was also from a Buddhist Bengali family in India, and he had studied and settled in Tucson, AZ, after finishing his PhD. We settled in Lexington, KY, with his new job and our three-month-old baby. For me, talking about anything emotional and painful was not socially acceptable or possible either at home or at work.

I cried regularly in the closet the first year and half after coming to the US, as I terribly missed my mother and friends. Calling via landline was quite expensive with no Skype, or WhatsApp. PTSD and immigration-related trauma is now well recognized in psychology. The immigration process can cause a variety of psychological problems related to negotiating loss and separation from country of origin, family members, and familiar food, customs and traditions, exposure to a new physical environment, and the need to navigate unfamiliar cultural expectations.

From my first two job experiences, I learned that the causes of alienation and suffering at workplaces was mainly due to ignorance and lack of skillfulness or empathy around identity, culture, emotional intelligence, and communication. Coming from the monsoon climate of Calcutta, India, in 1985, I had to leave my close-knit group of family and friends and quickly learned to adapt to the different physical, mental, and emotional climate of Tucson, Arizona, as a married, full-time graduate student with a somewhat confusing and complex relationship with in-laws. My own ignorance and lack of awareness around suffering of change, skillful communication, and emotional boundaries made things difficult and more painful.

Even in January 1993, as a young mother, I could see my ignorance of the all-pervading nature of the first noble truth of suffering as taught by the Buddha. The *samvega* I experienced was not just my pain but the pain of all people in my shared space and environment. From the streets of Calcutta, while commuting by bus to college and university for seven years, I witnessed the sheer poverty, homelessness, and hunger of millions unemployed, working at menial informal jobs and living in slums and unsafe squatters.

Awakening With Ease: going deeper

The next Seven Chapters deal with the six "A" step cultivations to transform one's habitual mind and conditioned behavior that keeps one trapped into one's own story of pain, victimization, despair, and disappointments, creating alienation from one's own self, life, and society. Our mind can fall asleep while going through the auto-pilot life at home and work, not being present with anything for most of the day.

The Awakening With Ease (AWE) method offers a simple six-step process which can be quickly remembered and put into practice easily. One can pick one step at a time and practice it for three to five weeks daily until a shift is felt or the next step unfolds naturally. It is always best to find a friend, support person, or sangha to keep you accountable and motivated initially. It is also relaxing for the body to go to a healing yoga retreat, body movement and detox program, or trauma-informed mindfulness retreat to restore balance in body, mind, emotion, and spirit, before engaging with serious meditation like a ten-day vipassana course. The more open, kind, and gentle you are with yourself, the more easily the process unfolds. Striving for a fixed outcome is a sure sign of craving coming from an egoic mind.

Awakening from the dream of *samsara*

For me, relaxing into present moment awareness unfolded easily as I observed my mind was swinging from past to future wildly. My mind was in a whirlpool current of some sort, repeating the memories of unpleasant events again and again, like a broken record. With strong intention, I resolved to unplug from the past and future and stay in the present by locking my open awareness focused on the body and bodily activities. When sitting and lying down I became aware of the breath, its nature, and qualities from gross to subtle and almost non-existent.

By simply noticing the breath, whole breath-body, and body sensations, both mind and body would become calm and serene. For the first time, I started feeling a happiness (bliss) infusing my body-mind I had not felt in a long time. This naturally changed to meditation on feelings and then mind itself. It blossomed into loving-kindness meditation of the four immeasurable divine states (*brahmaviharas*). The serenity prayer helped me set boundaries with regard to empathy and sensitivity to others and my own emotions.

"The whole path of mindfulness is this:
whatever you are doing be aware of it."
-Dipa Ma

The process of non-identification (not I, me, or mine) with the five aggregates of personality or name and form (*namarupa*)—form, feeling, perception, mental habits, and consciousness—was present from the second month. My concentration (*samadhi*) started deepening with *brahmaviharas* in the realm of form. Once equanimity was stable, I could see causes and conditions leading me to successive steps in mindful meditation. I also had the first inner glimpse of the four noble truths: recognition of suffering, its cause, its cessation, and the path leading to the end of ignorance and suffering. My last meditation was meditation on the six elements—earth, water, fire, air, space, and consciousness—when the boundary between body-mind and elements totally disappeared and mind became unshakable and indestructibly rooted in equanimity.

Contemplating on the six elements and their qualities and seeing them flow through our body-mind is a way to enter from the form to formless meditative absorptions (*jhana*) and profound contemplation on interconnectedness, impermanence, and insubstantiality of self. The unexpected sudden awakening to the unconditioned happened spontaneously after seven months of sustained mindfulness with strong deliberate resolve (*adhitthana*) to wake up. It climaxed into a week of deep unshakable mountain-like mental calm and tranquility without a single distractive thought. A thought-free empty awareness of immeasurable peace and equanimity (called the imperturbable state) arose after a sequence of meditations. It led to spontaneous stilling of all mental formations, perception, and feeling through non-clinging. It climaxed to an ecstatic joy of freedom and release of a wispy subtle energy through the crown into deep space, the void (*sunnya*).

> In Reality form is like "a lump of foam" (phenapinda); sensation like "a water bubble" (bubbula); perception like "a mirage" (marici); mental formations like "a plantain tree" (kadalik-khandha); and cognition is like "a magical illusion" (maya).
> –Phenapindūpama Sutta (SN 22:95)

This led to sudden cessation of a tiny bubble-like stream of consciousness and unbinding of the subtle five aggregates of self with a simultaneous blinking out of self and the world. This supramundane experience was far beyond the ordinary human stream of consciousness, language, and thought. As I came out of the samadhi (void) after about two hours (somehow my eyes fell on the clock before and after I went to bed) my inquiry was, where did the body come from? Instantly, there was a piercing broad beam of laser-like light from deep space, silent illumination, and a reflection of a radiant light-body appeared in the physical oval mirror in my own bedroom.

As I was witnessing on the physical mirror this reflection of a celestial androgynous figure (light-body) in a disembodied empty state, I was witnessing in awe and a subtle fear arose below the solar plexus with the bulging tummy of the light body with a silvery cord. And immediately there was a simultaneous return of consciousness with the body on the bed. I was left with a most profound sublime peace, wonder, awe, and cessation of all suffering.

This was followed by an experience of a powerful vibration and vortex of cosmic energy (like anti-gravity) in every particle in my body three days later. It was far beyond what can be expressed by ordinary human thought and language. It took me beyond all doubt, fear, suffering, and delusion of a separate suffering self that plagues most of humanity. A sense of sublime peace, wonder, and awe filled me for months after this. Awakening is an irreversible shift, a supramundane superconscious experience and tectonic shift in human consciousness that takes one beyond doubt about the non-physical spiritual nature of reality, mind, and self.

"We are spiritual beings having a human experience."
-Pierre Teilhard de Chardin.

A new paradigm of knowledge and vision gradually infused my conscious-awareness over the next seven years. After that luminous experience of liberation in 1993, I never felt the need for a spiritual path or teacher, yet to this day I do delight in spiritual friendship and practicing with different communities. All my worldly roles, attachments and identities as a woman, Indian, immigrant, Buddhist, professional, mom, spouse, sister, daughter, in-laws, aunt, neighbor, and such lost their hold in my consciousness.

I was doing all my worldly duties, but internally, I was in a twilight place between the non-physical and the physical for the next seven years. I had some visions and dreams of past lives, shamanic dreams (without consciously knowing anything about it), lucid dreams of flying, hollow earth, and past or perhaps parallel lives. I was forced to come down to the earthly realm in 1999, when both my mother-in law and young sister-in law died within a month due to Alzheimer's and childbirth.

Rohitassa and other suttas

In 2014, I began to study Pali *suttas* for the first time as part of my Dharmacharya Program. I tried to make sense of my life-changing experience in 1993 from early Buddhist texts. Certain passages stood out for me.

> "I tell you, friend, that it is not possible by traveling to know or see or reach a far end of the cosmos where one does not take birth, age, die, pass away, or reappear. But at the same time, I tell you that there is no making an end to suffering and stress without reaching the end of the cosmos. Yet it is just within this fathom-long body, with its perception and intellect, that I declare that there is the cosmos, the origination of the cosmos, the cessation of the cosmos, and the path of practice leading to the cessation of the cosmos."
>
> -Buddha to Deva Rohitassa AN 4.45

> "With the complete transcending of the dimension of neither perception nor non-perception, he enters and remains in the cessation of perception and feeling. And, having seen [that] with discernment, his fermentations are completely ended. This is called a monk who, coming to the end of the cosmos, remains at the end of the cosmos, having crossed over attachment in the cosmos."
>
> -Brahmana Sutta, AN 9.38

*"When ignorance is abandoned and true knowledge
has arisen in a bhikkhu, then with the fading away of
ignorance and the arising of true knowledge, he no longer
clings to sensual pleasures, no longer clings to views, no
longer clings to rules and observances, no longer clings
to a doctrine of self (attavāda). When he does not cling,
he is not agitated. When he is not agitated, he personally
attains Nibbana (completely unbound/calmed/pacified/
deathless).*

-Short sutta on Lion's Roar MN 11.17

Process of inquiry and intention

A deep reflection on what I truly love, and my true nature led me to a spiritual quest of my own. Some of my inquiry process went like this: Who am I not? This body I hold so dear is perishable. Survival of the body need not be my ultimate concern. What happens to mind consciousness after we die? How would I live my life in harmony with my own heart, doing what I love? What is my original nature and face before my other social identities as woman, Buddhist Bengali, daughter, mother, wife, in-laws, aunt, professional, academic, immigrant, Asian, heterosexual, and such lenses were superimposed? What is my own deepest need and the need of people and the planet now? What to abandon and what to cultivate so my mind is free from craving, fear, and limiting identity constructs?

*"Condemnation without investigation
is the height of arrogance."*

-Albert Einstein

In my self-discovery process, I saw that in my mind there was a clash of two cultures and cultural expectations. I was determined to find a way out to my own path to freedom, joy, and happiness. I must go beyond my own conditioning of culture, gender, social myths, validations, and external attachments. I slowly became my own island and refuge to know myself, my true work, and my purpose in this lifetime. I needed to wake up to new knowledge and inner vision to find my true North, by aligning my mind, body, emotions, and spirit. I became aware of internalized expectations of Indian culture in my marriage at home and also the Western cultural norms at work, like white supremacy thinking, toxic individualism, targeting vulnerable and POC, power hoarding, paternalism, disempowering women and minorities, internalized violence, lack of appreciation, empathy, biases, and stress.

Like many of you reading this, I went through what the Catholic author and Trappist monk, Thomas Merton, said here:

> *"The rush and pressure of modern life are a form, perhaps the most common form of its innate violence. To allow oneself to be carried away by a multitude of conflicting concerns, to surrender to too many demands, to commit oneself to too many projects, to want to help everyone in everything, is to succumb to violence."*

Plus, the many overlapping systems of oppression one has to negotiate and adapt to as a minority, woman, person of color, immigrant, and first-time mom in a different language and culture with different norms and stereotypes added to my own suffering of change. Looking back, suffering illuminated my path, and it will illuminate yours, too.

Longer story as an immigrant to the US

This deliberate mindful journey into awareness of the unseen and unknown started seven years after coming to the US in the fall of 1985 from Kolkata, India. I still remember the very hot, humid day of taking my first and longest flight (forty-four hours) to the Los Angeles Airport. I was accompanied by my mother and eldest brother to the Calcutta Airport. As we boarded the cab with two suitcases, several of our neighbors came out to their porch to see me off. Both my mom and I cried all the way to the airport. For me, this long journey felt like both an adventure and a caution. Flying away from the monsoon climate and home life in Calcutta, India, to homelessness in the blazing hot desert land of Tucson, Arizona, made me feel like a fish thrown out of its familiar lagoon.

Having never lived away from home, family, and friends before, my pain and anguish (*vedana*) of sudden loss of contact with my mother (widowed in 1981) was too much to bear at times. I missed and craved Bengali food, culture, language, and community for almost two and a half years. I could call home briefly once in a month or two, as calling via land line was expensive. It took twenty-eight months before my spouse and I could visit home in India after finishing my graduate studies at the University of Arizona. Standing in the LAX immigration line, the word "alien" captured my attention and made me somewhat apprehensive. A thought arose, *How can a human being from the same planet be an alien?*

Marriage, Work and Family

We had an unconventional marriage, and yes, it was arranged by me! I had a strong sense of my future spouse many years before I met him in India. We were both from the Barua Buddhist clan (see Wikipedia) of the Plain Buddhists in undivided India, who survived in Chittagong, Bangladesh, and the West Bengal area of India since ancient times. We were not practicing Buddhism beyond generosity and ethics, which kept us going despite difficulties of life as first-generation immigrants. After completing my masters in geography, I quit my PhD program, following my inner voice not to limit my life exploration with a narrow academic focus. I was also six months pregnant.

Raising our only child, Maya, after a difficult first trimester and C-section without the presence of a family and community around was the most psychologically daunting yet rewarding task we went through as immigrant parents. Surprisingly, simply observing Maya's every facial expression, tiny body movements, and interaction with other people and objects helped me connect with my own beginner's mind and heightened my own sense of gratitude for my parents. We had to sell our new home in Arizona and move to Kentucky due to my husband's new job, with our three-month-old colicky baby. Things went well for a while (inspite of initial sleepless nights and postpartum depression), until Maya was twenty-two months old, and I got my first full-time job as a socio-economic planner in the long-range city planning department. Here, I faced all kinds of culture-gender-age-related communication barriers and discrimination.

I was the only international (as I was in most of my graduate school experience) and only woman, in an all-male, dysfunctional, mostly white office environment. This added considerably to my stress and emotional alienation. As an empath and sensitive (which I learned a decade later), I was taking on everyone's pain in my office. I also absorbed a lot of pain from my mother-in-law, who had lost her spouse in an accident quite young and had to raise six children on her own. As if an inner alarm (Buddha called it *samvega*) was set off inside of me, I felt that if I didn't make a wise choice soon, I would either succumb to a serious illness or an accident. I paid close attention and quit my job and career to take the path less traveled, the path to the wise heart.

Myth of happiness

The prevailing cultural and social myth of happiness and well-being is based on the value of college education. Even with huge student debt-loads (an average of $37,000 as of 2022), college education is seen as the surefire way to freedom, success, and privilege in the modern world. By 1993, I had all the outward signs of success as a young professional mom trying to balance my work and personal lives. I did my best to get on board with the hedonic treadmill of adaptation in a culture very different than the one I left. I had the privilege of a nice suburban home with two cars and a mortgage, a bright kid, and an executive spouse with a PhD. Yet I ended up intensely unhappy and agitated inside, with painful ongoing discrimination at work, lack of empathy of people around me, uncertainty in my job and my spouse's corporate job, and my utter lack of motivation in continuing the daily business of living and working as usual.

"Our journey to find meaningful work can often lead us
on the journey to finding a meaningful life."
-Scott Schute, Author of Full Body Yes

Awakening (AWE) is also about waking up from various systems of internalized oppression in the fear-based old paradigm of patriarchy, religion, racism, sexism, homophobia, colonial mentality, and debt capitalism (look for my Tikkun article online). It is about recognizing and training our inherent faculty of awareness and turning our attention inward to wake up to a greater dimension of life that we long to connect with.

Awakening takes us to the source of all life, our very being, luminous mind and restores our connection with the cosmos. A reconnection to life at the source that is more alive, real, and aligned with one's true nature, passion, purpose, joy, and inner knowing. We must be willing to know the unknown and befriend our own mind and go through our own transformation by being willing to see, know, and accept reality as it is unfolding in this present moment within and around us and the next "now" moment.

Why I needed to write this

I wanted to share my discovery for the benefit of many. It was not easy as an outlier and a woman of color. Three times, I stopped writing this book as I tried to fit in different sanghas. However, there were a few spiritual friends (some non-Buddhist) who encouraged me to keep going. One fellow Dharmacharya friend, Margi, started calling me a noble one. My mother was the first to see the shift in me in the mid-1990s. She came to visit me and her grandchild from India to the US for the second time. As we were talking around kitchen table, she suddenly got up and touched my feet. It was so unusual and against the cultural norm that both of us were simultaneously amazed and embarrassed. Sometimes, a total stranger on a flight or a new connection would say something that would help me remember the power of recognition in untainted awareness. One of my elder monastic friends and mentors, Venerable Pannadipa, said "One may dig a thousand wells to find water and come up dry. You dug one and found water. You should stick to it." So here I am, writing it for you.

As an observer of life from a very early age, I am a natural authority-leader-teacher of my own life. This book is about a self-discovery process inspired by the Buddha into our true nature, and the interdependent nature of reality, mind, and self. What I teach you here is how to be a student of life, how to remember and not forget the experience of critical events in your life, how to listen to the whispers of your own heart, achieve heart brain coherence, and use both reason and intuition to find alignment with what you value and truly love, your passion to know and understand everything at a deeper level, find purpose and joy in serving others, by ending craving and ignorance so you can transcend, not only the pain of the human dimension, but also the pleasures of the human and divine dimensions to awaken to the ultimate freedom of the unconditioned *nirvana* (*nibbana* in Pali) without the involvement of ego-personality.

Internally, I felt alone as a new mom in a new city without the presence or support of parents or community. I could not share my daily stress and anxiety of packing up a sleeping child each morning along with a diaper bag and three lunch packs to jump in the van by 7:20 a.m. As professional parents, we did our best to rush through the morning traffic to leave our daughter with the babysitter to show up on time in a stressful environment in our downtown city and corporate offices. Five years after coming to the US, this reality was far from the dream life of opportunity, freedom, and happiness I envisioned. I was burned-out in only two years and decided to resign from my professional city planning job, mostly due to the stress of discrimination and biases.

As a first-generation immigrant, I had to quickly adapt to a new country and culture, food, clothing, environment, and belief systems very different from what I grew up with in Kolkata, India. I was unaware of the suffering of change and impermanence before I immigrated. My parents also must have gone through similar suffering while moving from the rural environment of Chittagong, East Pakistan (present Bangladesh), to the crowded city of Calcutta. My grandparents also relocated from Chittagong to Yangon, Burma, for a better life and were forced to return home after a decade or so.

Why this book and who it is for

This book is my offering for the post-COVID world where many people, especially young people, are suffering from unprecedented depression, self-alienation, addiction, hopelessness, and suicidal impulses. Many women and men are searching for stress relief, mental calm, economic safety, freedom from fear, a life of higher purpose, meaning, contribution, joy, and even awakening.

Awakening is a compelling calling for those who are walking the heart's path to wisdom, compassion, and enlightenment. To practice AWE, you do not need to change your faith or convert your lifestyle to monasticism. You can simply start with what makes you feel alive, safe, clean, accepting, aware, happy, loving, and joyful from within, without the need to please others or get external attention or approval.

This book is for professionals who are unhappy or dissatisfied with their job because they feel they are out of alignment with their inner compass or contributing less than 10% of what they are capable of. It's also for women, moms, indigenous people, immigrants and people of color who have always felt marginalized by the mainstream. There are many who have not felt seen or heard, although they have something important to contribute to the collective me-we paradigm of collaboration, peace and possibilities based on the wisdom of love, healing, non-harm, and fearless truth.

Had I come to the US in search of freedom, happiness, adventure, and discovery, or to gather experiential knowledge of what is real? Inside, though, I was looking for a cure to end human impoverishment, oppression and suffering I experienced during my daily bus commute to college for seven years in the highly congested streets of Calcutta, India.

Here's what that means for you

Happiness is a pleasant feeling. Any happiness driven by desire and sense pleasure that is fleeting and leads to harm in the end cannot be the source of true happiness. How much of our desires are driven by advertising, news, social media, and various manipulations and temptations?

"Mendicants, without giving up the underlying tendency to greed for pleasant feeling, without dispelling the underlying tendency to repulsion toward painful feeling, without eradicating ignorance in the case of neutral feeling, without giving up ignorance and without giving rise to knowledge, it's simply impossible to make an end to suffering in the present life."
-Buddha (Chachakka sutta)

The Buddha distinguished between two kinds of happiness: physical and mental happiness, material and spiritual happiness, happiness of laypeople and renunciates, happiness of sensual desire and renunciation, happiness of the noble and ignoble ones, happiness of attachment and non-attachment, defiled and undefiled happiness, and happiness of enjoyment and seclusion. The better of these two kinds of happiness is the second kind of happiness of the renunciates and four types of noble (*arya*) ones. Buddha also encouraged all people seeking happiness and safety to develop a mind of universal love (*metta*) and goodwill toward all beings and not to be afraid of good deeds.

What I understood from my own journey is that external success in education, job, marriage, and possession do not translate to inner peace, freedom, and happiness. I had no conscious recognition of the importance of a nurturing environment and self-care at home, work, relationships, and community network until years after I moved away from them from India to the US.

The American psychologist Abraham Maslow, in his Expanded Hierarchy of Needs, puts physical survival and safety as the basic need throughout life (in my view, especially after suffering due to job loss, accident, death, divorce, trauma, or undesirable change of environment).

"It isn't normal to know what we want. It is a rare and difficult psychological achievement….What a man can be, he must be. This need we call self-actualization."

–Abraham Maslow

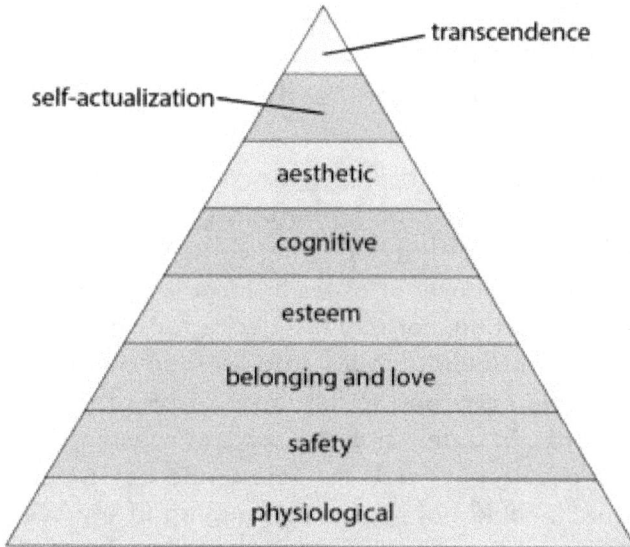

Image from Wikipedia

The social needs for love and belonging, self-esteem, autonomy, self-actualizing growth, engagement, and meaning are equally important for happiness and well-being. Some of the basic safety needs are job and financial security, health and wellness, and the need for self-esteem, which form the need for power, control, recognition from ego (healthy or unhealthy). Cognitive need is the need for curiosity, inquiry, meaning, predictability, understanding, and experimentation.

Maslow refined his 'hierarchy of needs" later in life by adding self-transcendence above self-actualization of creative talents. In self-transcendence one is motivated by values that go beyond personal self and one desires to connect with a higher reality, purpose or the universe. This level emphasizes altruism, spiritual connection and helping others achieve their potential. What I realized is that the suffering and awakening to life's ultimate purpose, i.e, self-transcendence can happen simultaneously with the recognition of any one or more of the basic human needs not being met in adult life.

Humans need beautiful imagery or something new like art, music, poetry, crafts, photography, or contact with the natural world that is aesthetically pleasing in search of beauty, balance, or order in form to continue up to self-actualization. For me, the desire for right-livelihood took me to a deeper inquiry into life and death, purpose of life, who I am, and mindfulness of breath-body and movements. In a new city and job environment, many of my psychological needs for safety and belonging were not met. I could not ignore the longing of my heart for solitude and seclusion.

"What is necessary to change a person is to change his awareness of himself."

-Abraham Maslow

How this book helps you as a leader

"Research shows, the habit of (self) reflection can separate extraordinary professionals from mediocre ones. We would go so far as to argue that it's the foundation that all other soft skills (empathy, communication, adaptability, emotional intelligence, compassion) grow from."
-Harvard Business Review, 03-2022

- You become more familiar with your own mind-body-speech habits and transform unskillful ones to skillful ones so you can better relate with your own mind and your team at work, home, and community. You rule by ruling your mind, becoming a person of integrity, leading by example, and adhering to the universal ethics of non-harm.

- The six "A" steps are designed to get you in touch with your direct experience of feeling and sensation in the body and to calm the body-mind to safely focus on what is needed for you, your partner, and your team to regain balance moving forward with self-acceptance, self-love, and compassion for all.

- What is the best action or non-action step right now, today, or in the next ten days? This mindful inquiry to be receptive of inner guidance will ground your practice with a focus.

- Develop more contentment, engagement, leadership presence, tolerance, and acceptance of other views, more empathy, emotional intelligence, and compassionate ways to relate with your network, supervisor, and sangha.

- More awareness, better communication, and right understanding of each other's needs, values, and vulnerabilities to work best in a team.

- Develop a personalized meditation and spiritual practice based on wise view, attention to present situation, and wise intention. Review, reflect, and make adjustments every seven weeks.

- This book is about self-leading your own way. Brene Brown, author of *Dare to Lead*, defines a leader as, "someone who takes responsibility for finding the potential in people and processes and who has the courage to develop those potentials." She says, "We desperately need more leaders who are committed to courageous, wholehearted leadership and who are self-aware enough to lead from their hearts, rather than unevolved leaders who lead from hurt and fear."

"A leader is one who knows the way, goes the way,
and shows the way."
-John Maxwell

What's going to happen in the world

As you, your friends, colleagues, and spontaneous AWE circles around the globe put into practice the Awakening With Ease steps, your life will start to sync and flow better, with less effort, more ease, success, and happiness. You will create a positive vibe at work and home environment where people bring their best, become spiritual friends, and support each other with a shared vision, mission, project, or outcome.

Everything in nature follows its nature and transforms by itself. As Lao Tzu said, "Nature does not hurry, yet everything is accomplished." With mindful presence you would also tune into your own nature, natural inclinations, gifts, and skills so you are in harmony with all things and people in your environment. As we begin to trust life and our own nature, we can let things be for now and not rush into things beyond our control. With continued practice, it is easier to let go of fear and resistance to the present moment, seize the moment, and be in the flow. Cultivating the four establishments of mindfulness of body, feeling, mind, and *dharma* principles is the way to develop calm and insight to cope with what Buddha called "*the suffering of change and reactive mind habits (sankhara)*".

What's going to happen in the workplace when more and more people practice AWE?

Recognition of many sources of workplace stress, disengagement, and burnout is the first step. It takes just one caring person and a volunteer to start a simple mindfulness program or AWE Circle in the workplace. Our body's circadian rhythms are based on physical, mental, behavioral, and hormonal changes that follow an approximately twenty-four-hour cycle in tune with daylight. Simple mindfulness practices can bring awareness and support to our body-mind's internal clock and increase well-being, engagement, and productivity from the inside.

What would happen in communities with race, gender, and cultural diversity when more people put the practice of Awakening With Ease into place?

Our sense of trust, safety, solidarity, resilience, cooperation, and mutual support is likely to increase in communities that gather regularly in spaces for mindful study, practice, and dialogue groups. Building intentional communities of solidarity and resilience and co-housing is the best antidote for our increasingly complex, diverse, and divided world in the fast, post-modern, technology-driven, virtual global culture.

As we recognize and acknowledge our common humanity and empathy for traumatic human experiences around race, gender, culture, class, non-binary orientation, and such around safe spaces with secular practice of mindful meditation, we can renew and recreate our relations, heal the ancestral pain, anger, trauma, and fear of "the other" that is not ultimately true. This can start at schools, neighborhoods, public spaces, and institutions with a few people of compassion.

What might happen for your business and your ideal client if a few of the Awakening With Ease practices are incorporated into you weekly work schedule and your formal and informal business meetings and best practices?

There are many studies done at the workplace about the tangible and sustainable impact of mindfulness practices on employee health and happiness, increased work-life balance, reduced employee stress, improved performance, and enhanced engagement. Mindfulness practices have been used in many corporate environments to improve leadership trust, calm, and focus, creativity, performance, empathy, emotional intelligence, better communication, and compassion. Some early adopters include Google, Apple, General

Mills, Intel, Aetna, SAP, Cisco, Nike, Fidelity, Goldman Sachs, and AstraZeneca, and the list is growing.

Following the steps of The Noble Tenfold Path (The Noble Eightfold Path is actually tenfold with the last two outcome stages of right knowledge and vision, and nirvana or right liberation), in my opinion, is the path for evolutionary leaders, guardians, and changemakers who are deeply engaged to change the global and planetary systems from the inside out. We need awareness-based tools for mindful system change in self, society, economics, government, and new paradigm institutions based on universal generosity, ethics, love, mindful-meditation, non-conceptual knowledge, and wisdom.

CHAPTER 2

Know Your Why and Your Story

❦

"The breeze at dawn has secrets to tell you. You must ask for what you really want. Don't go back to sleep"

-Rumi

"Sole dominion over the earth, going to heaven, mastery over all worlds, the fruit of stream entry excels them."

-Dhammapada 178

Here's why this is important

Awakened beings feel called to serve the deepest needs of the planet and people in times of great transformation and change. They use their inherent awareness-based wisdom, compassion, intuition, and spiritual sensitivity to rise above unhealthy egoic needs of survival, alienation, greed, fear, suspicion, jealousy, competition, war, control, and power over others. Such wise beings provide a cool shade, a lamp, a quiet refuge, a wise way out of the collective pain, suffering, and ignorance for many.

Dharma is an ancient Indian thought (*Bharatiya* idea) that does not mean religion (in the sense of institutionalized spiritual beliefs). The root word of *dharma* is *"dhr,"* which means to uphold, to support, and sustain existence according to the *dharma* (true nature of things, natural universal principle, or nature of reality) of phenomena. To live the *dharma* life is to gain wisdom, self-knowledge, and spiritual awakening and is the primary and ultimate purpose of human life. Pursuit of worldly wealth, power, and pleasure are secondary goals.

What is the benefit and for whom

The term "ārya" is often found in many *dharma* traditions of India, like the Vedic Sanatana Dharma, Buddha Dharma, Jain, Sikh, Arya Samaj, and Brahmo Samaj Dharma texts. The many spiritual faith traditions of India aimed at cultivation and liberation of the human mind are sometimes collectively called ārya *dharma*(s). "Arya" refers to the honorable or noble ones who upheld or sustained true dharma in the place called "aryavarta" (abode of *aryas*) or the Northern Gangetic and Indus Plain between the Himalayas and Vindya Mountain of India. The ancient universal, humanistic, and spiritual ideals of Arya Dharma have been lost and degenerated many times through many complex and conflicting forces of history.

Why it is important

There are three or four kinds of enlightened beings, like the historical Sammasam Buddha, Paccekabuddhas (solitary individual Buddhas), Arahants, and Arya Bodhisattvas. The first two kinds of beings discover the ancient direct path to awakening on their own and the last two through hearing the teaching of Buddhas and enlightened teachers. Buddha reframed the notion of *dharma* from duty and obligation (to gods, ancestors, scriptures) to personal observation of *dharma* (phenomena) into your own nature and investigation of the nature of reality (*dharma*) through your direct perception and experiential realization. In that sense, *dharma* is a spiritual non-physical science of the heart-mind (citta), consciousness (vijnana) and manas (thinking and mental formations that cling to memory).

A little history and language on enlightenment

This book uses the word "enlightenment" in the sense of spiritual awakening, *bodhi*, and illumination of the human consciousness. According to Wikipedia, *The Oxford English Dictionary* credits the first recorded use of the term "enlightenment" to the Journal of the Asiatic Society of Bengal (February 1836). The Times used the term "the Enlightened" for the Buddha in a short article in 1857, which was reprinted the following year by Friedrich Max Müller, a German-born Indologist, orientalist, and philologist who lived and worked mostly in Britain.

The word "enlightened" comes from the Latin prefix "en" meaning "in or into" and the word "lux" meaning "light." Combine these meanings—into the light—and you describe what it is that characterizes an enlightened person: a sense of profound clarity, connection, illumination, sublime peace, perfect liberation (*nibbana*), and a profound realization of the nature of reality, mind, and self as void or *sunyata*. To contextualize the importance of spiritual awakening in

Western culture, we need to ground it in modern language and emerging scientific world views.

The Age of Enlightenment was an intellectual, political, and philosophical movement that dominated Europe in the 17th and 18th centuries until the end of the Napoleonic War in 1815, with defining concepts such as the use of reason and the scientific method for the pursuit of knowledge, human happiness, freedom, progress, separation of church and state, secular education, democratic constitution and freedom of speech, thinking, alongwith worldwide influences and colonization, slavery, racism, and sexism.

Forces of darkness and light co-existed throughout human history. Much of our history was written by the victor or colonizing country, undergoing revisions by independent researchers and alternative historians. Truth is the first casualty in any kind of war, including wars on drugs, terrorism, market share, and pre-emptive national war.

Bridging enlightened society, self and citizens

It must be noted here that there was a parallel and unenlightened history of colonialism, slavery, racism, sexism, capitalism that continued along with the age of European enlightenment. In the process of colonization, colonizers imposed their religion, language, economics, and legal-political system of exploitation, not to mention the massive looting, plunder, psychological damage, divide, and rule policies creating ethnic-religious tensions, famine, outrageous atrocities, and denial of democracy (Sashi Tharoor 2018).

In our current digital information age, we are bombarded with information from news and social media, smartphone texts, and pop-up advertising. Only a tiny fraction of it is useful information and knowledge. Knowledge is not useful until you can process and apply it. There are potential harmful effects of the hijacking of attention by computers and artificial intelligence. They trigger heightened attention-deficit symptoms, technology addiction, social isolation, impaired social-emotional intelligence, disrupted sleep, impaired brain development, and an adverse impact on relationships at home and work.

What is the benefit and for whom

Over 2,600 years ago, Buddha showed mankind the escape route from the socially conditioned mind-matrix based on greed, stress, fear, anxiety, addiction, hate, violence, and ignorance. He said human life is precious and the mind is our most important asset in life. We need to be mindful and vigilant in cultivating good qualities of our mind by sowing good seeds of thought, intent, word, and action, plus also guard and protect our hearts from greed, anger, jealousy, pride, lies, and other such poison that distort our view and conduct. We have the capacity to establish an island of sanity, calm, resilience, and peace within this mind-body to offer safety and support to us and those around us.

Benefits of awakening (enlightenment)

- Sublime peace, ultimate knowledge, wisdom, truth
- Freedom from fear of death and uncertainty

- A profound clarity, knowing beyond doubt, coming home
- Direct insight into the nature of reality, universal mind, not-self
- Realizing ultimate truth, unconditioned, unborn, *sunnyata*
- Irreversible shift in consciousness, wholeness, and healing
- Embodiment of love, compassion, joy, and equanimity
- Awakened power of presence, simplicity, wise action
- End of greed, rage, hate, delusion, conceit, envy, guilt, shame
- Self-discovery of the middle way to knowledge and vision
- From chaos, confusion to coherence, clarity, conviction
- End of worldly desire for gain, fame, pleasure, validation
- Freedom from the matrix of painful mind habits, prejudice, and myths
- Return to luminous source, emptiness, pure consciousness
- End of *karma*, rebirth, death, wheel of *samsara*
- Cooling off the fire of greed, hate, delusion of ego-identity
- Return to authentic power, sovereignty, total trust in *dhamma*
- Disciplined mind, generous heart, benevolent engagements
- Profound equanimity, unshakable peace regardless of situation
- Inner paradigm shift helps humanity ascend without war

In Hopi lore, the butterfly is the symbol of human spiritual transformation and awakening. There comes a stage of development in a caterpillar's life when it creates a chrysalis around itself to enter darkness. Within the chrysalis, the body of the caterpillar undergoes transformation to become a butterfly. The capacity, worldview, and experience of the butterfly is completely different from that of the caterpillar.

To wake up, we need to plant the seed of awakening in our own consciousness and be the change we want to see in the world. We cannot change the old paradigm of greed, scarcity, domination, control, racism, and war without shifting our own mindset and worldview.

"We cannot solve our problems with the same thinking we used when we created them."
-Albert Einstein

"In order to change an existing paradigm, you do not struggle to try to change the problematic model. You create a new model and make the old one obsolete."
-Buckminster Fuller

The purpose of Buddhist observation of our everyday human experience (mindfulness) is to alleviate suffering, particularly the kinds created by stress, anxiety, anger, desire, envy, loneliness, anguish of unexpected change, and all-pervasive grief for the collective suffering in the planet. These affiliative emotions (*kleshas*) cloud the mind, producing distorted perceptions and unwholesome mental grasping, harsh speech, and harmful actions. Buddha observed his own mind and conditioning and directed it persistently to the problem of all-pervasive human suffering and found an irreversible way out of it. He never asked others to take his teaching as absolute but invited all to investigate it.

I did just that after being discriminated against in my first full-time job in an all-male environment as city planner and was glad I had the courage to unplug from my career and identity-view. As a mother of a young child, I returned home to take care of myself and her. I reflected on life and my part in it. I listened to my own heart after relaxing with my breath-body, followed my own intuition, and remembered those childhood wakeful moments and pilgrimage to Buddhist sites in my pre-teen and teen years, and the ancient Aryan path unfolded on its own.

I took it as an experiment and an inner adventure or game of some sort with a faint knowing, yet I was willing to die to my old self. This book is an invitation for you to access your heart's path for your ultimate liberation.

A simple foundation for happiness

The Oxford English Dictionary defines the American dream as "the ideal that every citizen of the United States should have an equal opportunity to achieve success and prosperity through hard work, determination, and initiative." Historically, however, the phrase represented the idealism of the great American experiment, says Professor Sarah Churchwell, author of *Behold America*.

James Truslow Adams, an American historian coined the term "American Dream" in his 1931 book, *The Epic of America*. He described the true American dream as "a genuine individual search and striving for the abiding values of life" and for "the common man to rise to full stature" in the free realms of "communal, spiritual, and intellectual life". I loved the American parks, forests, arboretums, and libraries as my sanctuary when I lost faith in conventional living. I am not alone in this. *Inc.com* reports that in June 2022, four million Americans left their jobs, with 10 million jobs available.

I started questioning this whole social myth that happiness comes from external validations, jobs, things, people, places, money, or material stuff. I remembered calm mental states of peace, happiness, and joy from my early childhood and pre-teen years without any of the stuff that became a necessity (or rather, baggage) later. I had an immediate recognition from my mental state that my twenty-plus years of formal education did not teach me anything on mind or mental development for happiness.

Imagine if every teacher, parent, expert, and scientist in any field learns how to take a pause, turn inward to calm themselves in moments of stress, anxiety, and frustration and shifts that to a slightly better place, day by day and moment by moment. Would their children, students, and clients have a happier life and relationship?

Buddhist psychology emphasizes the cultivation of positivity and letting go of negative mental states. It also emphasizes rubbing off the neurotic attachment to self. This is done by four contemplations of body, feeling, mind, and *dhamma* (*satipatthana*). Settling gently into your breath, body, heart-mind, and solitude for ten to fifteen minutes can be so centering, calming, and relaxing that it surprises some beginner students of mindfulness. You discover there is a natural well of happiness and joy in your own being that is not dependent on any external attention or validation.

What this means for you is

Use your limited time, attention, energy, and resources in life wisely before you are pulled away in multiple distractions. Learn the difference between the essential and inessential things in life so you can dwell in the field of wise attention and right intention. Mindfulness helps you discover your true nature.

> *"Trying to be what you are not, expends all your energy.*
> *Being what you are doesn't require any effort."*
> *-Don Miguel Ruiz*

> *"Those who consider the unessential to be essential*
> *And see the essential to be unessential,*
> *never arrive at the essential*
> *Dwelling in the field of wrong intention"*
> *-Dhammapada; ch 1:11*

Gift from a stranger

One aspect of awareness or mindfulness (*sati* in Pali, *smriti* in Sanskrit) is clear comprehension (*sampajanna*). It is about remembering and not forgetting your own life journey, wakeful moments, and events experienced with not only clear awareness but clear comprehension. I still recall the great joy I felt when I got an unexpected birthday gift from my father's new friend who was a publisher of children's books. It was a huge and heavy book titled, *The Children's Book of Knowledge.* This book opened my mind's horizon in directions like world history, philosophy, geography, science, biology, religions, literature, culture, economy, politics, and more.

My father was a great believer in having a good education to be successful and happy in life. I was not so sure about transferring from home to public school in third grade. I had an inquiry arise within me about education, knowledge, and the goal of life. Who should I take as my role model? Einstein and the path of inquiry of science or Buddha and the inquiry of the heart or spirit? Other thoughts arose in me. Science is directed toward investigation of the external, five-sensory world of form, and Buddha is looking within the internal world of the heart-mind or sixth sense. Which sense is primary? In my heart, I leaned toward Buddha, knowing fully well higher education is inclined toward science and Buddha's teaching has almost disappeared from India.

Learning within family

Once my father hosted a big birthday party (my only one) when I was three and invited all my teachers, friends, and neighbors. I got a lot of attention and nice presents. I could see how much of a sacrifice the celebration was for him; how many moments of hard work as a bachelor student and a married spouse had brought him to that moment. At that moment, I gave myself a suggestion to always remember how much my parents loved me. This is the first and earliest memory of making a right intention that I remember.

Once, I tried to win prizes in neighborhood sport events for kids for my mother out of gratitude and later from the seventh grade onward, I exerted myself to do well in school to make my father happy. Soon afterward, I recall the first Buddhist Sanghadana ceremony where five and more Buddhist monks were invited in our home from Dharmankur Vihara, which my great-grandfather Kripasaran has founded in 1892. It coincided with our (my sister and my) ear-piercing ceremony. I tried to run away and hide from this ceremony but had to give in to honor the monks invited for this cultural practice. My sister just followed me. We both surprised our parents and our school principal by graduating summa cum laude, both ranking first in our Secondary Board Exam from our neighborhood school for girls.

Dream of hunger, pain, and death

Around ages six and seven, I had two dreams and one death in our extended family that made an imprint on my psyche. In the first dream, I was writhing in pain and woke up with extreme, visceral pain in my stomach. My mother woke up in the next room and immediately brought me some food to relieve the pain. This was my first experience of extreme physical pain that I recognized as hunger. I'm not sure whether my mother forgot to feed me, or I neglected to eat. At the time, Mother was shocked and heart-broken to get the telegram of her dearest father's sudden death by stroke in Chittagong far away from Calcutta. For a few days, she could not suppress her grief, and I could hear her loud wails at night, two rooms away. As the eldest and only daughter my mom was adored by her father.

In the second dream, I was climbing up the stairs of some mansion, and suddenly a dog bit my right leg. I tried to wiggle my foot out of the dog's mouth but could not get free. I woke up with severe, numbing pain in my leg that lasted several minutes. I had a sudden *dhamma* insight and knew that this daytime waking life was a continuation of dream life. I developed a fear of dogs after my eldest brother was bitten three times by street dogs and had to take many painful shots with long needle near his navel. I wonder if my dream of a dog bite actually coincided with a similar incident around Dipama's real life far away in Burma.

Enigma of eldest son (sibling)

My eldest brother, Shyam, was born premature and almost died but was saved by the prolonged care of my grandmother. She herself lost two of her own infant sons after my mother was born, then had three other sons who survived. My mother felt she was not loved by her mom, but her dad (my grandpa) loved her unconditionally. I am not sure what karmic ties my own parents had with their eldest child; it was utterly exhausting, scary, and painful for them as long as they lived. By age sixteen, my eldest brother ran away from boarding school and from home many times. As a young boy, he was good at locating and killing poisonous snakes like cobras, and our neighbors would call on him for all kinds of emergency help. This was my first exposure to the sad impact of my bother's impulsive habits and later addiction that caused much pain (*dukkha*) within the family.

After several complaints from neighbors about my eldest brother's transgressions, one day I found my father losing his restraint and beating my brother black and blue. I was barely five and felt helpless yet mustered enough courage to intervene to restrain my father from beating Shyam. Surprisingly, my father stopped and went back to his room. Fifteen years later, he confided to me that something shifted within him that day, and he thanked me for that. My brother's impulsive, addictive, and wild risk-taking nature was a source of great anguish, concern, and shame, not only for my parents, but for us siblings as well. He probably had undiagnosed mental health issues and died of a sudden stroke at age fifty. My sister survived a near-fatal pneumonia at age eleven, and I saw firsthand how much both my parents sacrificed to save her life.

Even today, mental health problems are not recognized, diagnosed, or given appropriate attention in India. Yet, at times my dear brother exhibited a brave and generous heart, a humorous, artistic, extroverted, and adorable side that endeared him to many. My unspoken thought was, *how do virtuous and kind parents like ours end up with a child like my brother.* The Buddhist view of karmic tendencies (*sankhara*) that transfers from past lives was quite self-evident to me. Watching my father's physical health and eldest brother's mental health decline helped me develop more compassion for sickness and addiction. My mother also suffered from rheumatism and constant pain in her back, hip, and knees. By the time I was twenty-one, when my father passed away, I had learned firsthand about aging, sickness, and death as part of the human condition.

Change is sudden and unexpected

The year 1970-71 was a very dangerous time politically with the violent Naxalite Communist Movement erupting in West Bengal and a huge refugee influx in Calcutta from the Bangladesh War of Independence. One evening, while returning from the office, my father came running home in panic. He narrowly escaped an ambush attack on his life as all public officials had become a target of the violent, student Naxalites enlisted from the colleges of Calcutta.

My brother was recruited by the left-wing Naxalite-Maoist Student Group to paint and post party signs and posters on walls. Fearing for the boys' lives, my father got both my brothers admitted to a reputable boarding school at R.K. Mission Narendrapur. Meanwhile, three of my young uncles survived the Rajakar (East Pakistan militia group) attack in Chittagong and arrived in our house in Calcutta. They had soiled clothes, red eyes, and dysentery after a long dangerous escape on foot through forested hill tracts. My mother's compassion and constant care saved them all.

Insights from travel and pilgrimage

Our most memorable first family trip was to the peaceful beach of Digha, not far from Calcutta, bordered by beautiful groves of Casuarina pine trees. My interest in visiting the beach was heightened when my teacher described the ocean to me and said, "You cannot see the other shore." Immediately, a wish to see the other shore was planted within me. As our big tour bus got nearer, all my senses perked up and expanded. I could feel and hear the distant waves in my inner ear and smell the salty air miles away. When we finally arrived at the beach, I was silent and speechless with wonder and joy. It was my first experience of rapture and joy, the instant recognition of a cosmos much bigger than my backyard. A most strange yet wonderful feeling of oneness and an expansion and merging of inner and outer space of awareness happened!

This was the seed for what I would later call "Awakening With Ease," which you'll learn how to practice in this book. Our first family trip to Rajgir, Nalanda, Bodhgaya, and Sarnath in 1970, around age 10, made me, not only curious about Buddha's life and mission, but quite aware of some of the heart-felt experiences I had. My father invited my widowed grandma to come to visit us from Chittagong and accompanied us on this pilgrimage. My father took great care of my grandma (after she lost her husband). He paid for all her expenses to spend a month at Rajgir so she could heal and get relief from her arthritis from the hot-spring bathhouse there.

Climbing up the steps of Vulture Peak (*Gridjhakuta*) was a new and difficult experience for grandma and me. I was in awe that Buddha stayed many times on this hilltop and spoke to Sariputta and five hundred monks there. While climbing up took a lot of effort, getting down was quite easy. As I ran down the steps feeling light and joyful, I had this great urge to take a leap and fly like a giant bird from the peak. Twenty-three years later, I used this insight of balancing effort and effortlessness to forge my own middle way of practice.

As our rented white car brought us to the gate of the Office of Nalanda University, a very ordinary looking humble man (known to my father) came with a smile and enthusiasm to open the iron gate for our car to enter. My father said to us, "That is an enlightened man!" I was a bit dumbfounded yet believed my father, who was well respected as a man of foresight and integrity in our community. Watching the great ruin of Nalanda (427–1197 CE) made me see the impermanence of all things, even great historic monuments and institutions do not last forever.

What this means for you

Do you remember moments alone with yourself, your earliest memories of travel outside your home, your sensory memories of feeling alive, joyful, carefree, and happy for no reason? Do you recall having glimpses of space or a sudden expansion of your awareness or a sense of oneness with your environment? These moments are imprinted in your physical and cellular memory. You can bring them to your practice of awareness of four establishments of mindfulness. Also, bring your childlike curiosity and wonder to go behind your thoughts and feelings and observe them floating by with no identification, only presence of loving awareness. Remember to focus more on real contact with life experience and sense perceptions now, than any imaginary objects, concepts or fantasy thoughts that take you away from the present moment.

Part II

Six "A"s for Awakening with Ease

"Just as the dawn is the forerunner and first indication of the rising of the sun, so is the right (wholesome, true and wise) view the forerunner and first indication of wholesome states. For one of right view, monks, right intention springs up. For one of right intention, right speech springs up. For one of right speech, right action springs up. For one of right action, right livelihood springs up. For one of right livelihood, right effort springs up. For one of right effort, right mindfulness springs up. For one of right mindfulness, right concentration springs up. For one of right concentration, right knowledge springs up. For one of right knowledge, right deliverance of spirit."

—AN 10:121

"And what is the right view that is noble, without effluents, transcendent, a factor of the path? The discernment, the faculty of discernment, the strength of discernment, analysis of qualities as a factor for awakening, the path factor of right view in one developing the noble path whose mind is noble, whose mind is without effluents, who is fully possessed of the noble path. This is the right view that is noble, without effluents, transcendent, a factor of the path."

-MN 117

CHAPTER 3

Alive

"Love is the bridge between you and everything."
-Rumi

"We live in the world, when we love it."
-Tagore

"Better than one hundred years lived with an unsettled mind,
devoid of virtue, is one day lived virtuously and
absorbed in meditation."
-Buddha.

This and next few chapters describe the six foundational "A" steps needed to Awaken With Ease. These steps can be seen as a gradual, momentum-building process to develop the mind, its primary attitude and inclination. These steps (combination keys) also help us grow personally, professionally, and socially by seeing things deeply with clarity, by listening to our own body-mind-speech patterns, habits, and choices without condemnation. Our life is precious but limited. We can only make the best use of our time, energy, attention, and resources by living fully now, being alive (sajiva), connected and present with every person, situation, and task on a daily basis. Aliveness connects us with our breath and the direct experience and contact of the senses (*vedana*) with the natural and human world. Awakening is non-conceptual and experiential.

Aliveness is acknowledged by simply noticing our self-breathing body breathing itself. Simply place your hand over your beating heart and feel the warmth or coolness of breath-life energy flowing effortlessly through the body-mind sensations and feelings. Extend the same awareness of this life energy, prana, or chi in all sentient living beings. Feel the connection with nature and all beings in the interconnected web of life.

Aliveness is the natural movement of life energy and spirit within all beings we share the planet with. Being alive is synonymous with being aware, conscious, alert, mindful, and animated, along with moving, receptivity, openness, sensitivity, exuberance, and the capacity to react or respond to the environment with spontaneity, cheerfulness, vitality, growth, change, decay, death, and regeneration. We all come with limited life spans and energy. Manage this energy well by putting attention to things that make you alive and fresh, your lifestyle, food, drinks, your overall physical and mental health, and well-being.

The Dalai Lama, when asked what surprised him most about humanity, said:

"Man! Because he sacrifices his health to make money. Then he sacrifices money to recuperate his health. And then he is so anxious about the future that he does not enjoy the present; the result being that he does not live in the present or the future; he lives as if he is never going to die, and then dies having never really lived."

I know exactly what the Dalai Lama meant because I have seen it unfold in my own father's life. Life becomes dull, boring, anxious, and depressing when we are living in our thinking bubble and not fully present in our daily action and interaction.

After two years of struggle in an unhappy job as a city planner, I decided to take the risk of resigning from my job to restore my calm and raise our only child with sanity. At the time, I had all kinds of raging thoughts going in loops with conflicting emotions. My state of agitation came like a sudden cyclone out of nowhere. I was in a state of shock, dismay, and urgency for not finding the happiness the conventional life promises after accomplishing its goals.

Recently, I found the word "samvega" in early Buddhist literature and Bhikkhu Thanissaro, describing this inner agitated state of *samvega* as a state of dismay, shock, and spiritual urgency about the purpose of life and desire for liberation to escape the suffering of *samsara*. I had a premonition that if I did not take care of this intense emotional state, I would have an accident or experience prolonged illness. It is known that diamonds are formed under extreme pressure and temperature. The energy behind the emotion of *samvega* can be directed by wise attention and awareness toward liberation, inner illumination, and awakening.

What this means to you is

Remember the moments, people, places, and things that you felt most alive, joyful, fun, interesting and playful when you go through *samvega*. Those moments you can still feel and recall in your heart and cellular memory. The practice of aliveness can gently bring you to the present moment and let go of past hurts and future worries. Bring you more in the body and sensory awareness, away from the head and useless repeated thinking. Just remain curious about the intimacy you feel with your own experience. You will stop looking for external attention and validation. Slowly, this inward focus will help you discover your inner nature, authentic self, and natural talents. Some early life inquiries and interests that were never addressed in your long years of schooling and cultural conditioning may surface. Pay attention to these soft whispers.

From depression and grief to aliveness now

Many of us lose touch with how free, innocent and spontaneous we were as children, as we get caught up with existential struggles of living in adult life. We get domesticated, programmed and conditioned by many spoken and unspoken survival and fear-based beliefs from society, religion, parents, teachers, authority figures and their beliefs, rules and expectations about us, plus serious trauma for many (personal and ancestral). So we start to search for our authentic whole self, heal our old wounds, self-limiting views, and disconnection from our true nature. Just connecting with breath and full body awareness gently help us work through and let go of all the filters and defilements we may have accumulated unconsciously on the path to heart.

We know for certain we are alive when we are mindful of our breath and breathing body. When mindfulness of in-and-out breathing (Anapanasati sutta MN 161) is developed and pursued in a systematic way, even one's final in-breaths and out-breaths are known as they cease, not unknown (Maha Rahulovada sutta MN 62). The practice of coming to the body, sensation, and contact or feeling of six-senses brings us from conceptual mind of thinking to the reality of experience now.

> The flower speaks
> Blessed am I, blessed am I
> Upon this earth
> I took my birth inside the dust
> Kindly let me forget that
> Let me forget that
> There is no dirt at all
> No taint at all
> Inside my heart!

Here the poet Rabindranath Tagore inspires us to look within our pure heart, our precious human birth.

> "Mindfulness is love."
> -Dipa Ma

> "When love meets pain, it becomes compassion.
> When love meets happiness, it becomes joy. Joy
> is an expression of the awakened heart, a quality
> of enlightenment. When we live in the present, joy
> often arises for no reason. This is the happiness of
> consciousness that is not dependent on particular
> conditions. Children know this."
> -Jack Kornfield.

There is a huge number of people in the US suffering from depression, suicidal thoughts, and even attempted suicide, especially for young people after the pandemic. The Buddha taught that impermanence (change) is one of the three universal characteristics of life and existence. Everything changes, yet our mind hates change and expects things to last permanently, so we can feel stable and secure. We constantly forget our inevitable death and impermanence and fixate on people and things to remain the same. Our attention is split and hijacked from the present moment by all kinds of distractions, past memories, future concerns, social media, and technology.

> The mind hard to see,
> Subtle - alighting where it wishes -
> Far ranging,
> Solitary, incorporeal and hidden
> Is the mind.
> Those who restrain it,
> Will be freed from Mara's bond.
>
> -Dhammapada 3:36-37

> Whatever an enemy may do to an enemy,
> Or haters, one to another
> Far worse is the harm
> From one's own wrongly directed mind.
> Neither mother, nor father,
> Nor any other relative can do
> One as much good
> As one's own well-directed mind.
>
> -Dhammapada 3:42-43

If we are honest, we can see that we really are not present with life and with spouse, kids, friends, pets, and relatives with the little free times we have with them. Growing old, losing a loved one, getting fired, divorced, meeting with an accident or suffering an unexpected financial loss can and does happen without notice at inconvenient times. Contemplating regularly on impermanence and change actually helps us relax, let go, let be, heal our fearful emotions, develop resilience, and embrace now with an open mind and heart.

Presence in daily chores

> *"The whole path of mindfulness is this: Whatever you are doing, be aware of it. If everything is noted, all your emotional difficulties will disappear. When you feel happy, don't get involved in happiness. When you feel sad, don't get involved with it. Whatever comes, don't worry, just be aware of it."*
>
> -Dipa Ma

We have many opportunities to practice mindful presence in our daily lives. Presence is an important part of sustaining mindful-awareness in movement through daily chores. Simply bring the awareness and attention over the body in all four positions—sitting, walking, standing, and lying down—and relax into whatever chore you are doing. If it is listening to soft music, playing with kids or a pet, taking a walk in the garden or local park, doing movement exercise like tai chi, yoga, or dance, and connecting with good friends, even cooking, cleaning, eating, drinking coffee, taking a shower, or mowing the lawn—just bring your attention to the body and relax into the activity fully. Use your five senses more mindfully to sense things to anchor, calm, and ground yourself to your whole breath-body.

Every time mind goes to thinking, in the past or future, notice it and come back to the body and the activity. See how it feels. Done property one is likely to feel calmer, relaxed, happy, and balanced in body-mind. It is the nature of all living things to be alive both in motion and rest. You can see and experience life outdoors in nature. Your mind can become one with the gentle movement of water, rain, and snow, movement of the stars, a sunrise, or floating clouds in an empty sky. When you recognize and practice, the aliveness within, you naturally become calm. You can access your authentic spontaneous nature instead of habitual fight, flight, freeze, or fawn reaction to stress.

You have as much right to exist as any other living creature on the planet as long as you are breathing. Aliveness also has to do with progressive alignment of mind-body-emotion-spirit. This alignment can be achieved by systematic study, contemplation, and meditation on 37 Wings to Awakening, as taught by the Buddha. Quenching the fire of greed, hate, fear, and ignorance is the final goal of the Buddha's path to awakening.

What this means to you is

Recognize and accept your unskillful habits in body-mind-speech that drain your energy and the energy of those around you. Develop a strategy to practice the antidote of the negative habits like anger and ill will. Overcome fear with friendliness, greed with generosity, and craziness with self-restraint. If you crave food at a party, stand at the back of the line, take small portions, and eat mindfully. If you habitually dominate conversations in a group, practice deep listening and be curious about others. Restrain habitual anger with kindness, harsh speech with gentle speech, self-denial with self-care, and cruelty with compassion. See if you feel empowered and energized by your power to choose wisely.

Samvega to pasada is possible

Samvega is a complex cluster of thought and unpleasant emotion that is difficult to describe in English. Bhikkhu Thanissaro describes it as at least three clusters of feelings at once. It is the oppressive sense of shock. It is dismay that comes with realizing the futility and meaninglessness of the human experience in conventional living. When I experienced discrimination and inequality in both my culture and my first professional job after four years in two graduate schools, I immediately sensed the meaninglessness of it all. My spiritual path began with the intention to understand and get out of this painful stress of *samvega* and be happy and alive again.

Pasada is another complex set of wholesome feelings usually translated as "clarity and serene confidence" that develops through mindfulness or presence. It arises from connecting and listening to the heart's intuitive wisdom and knowing that there is a way out of suffering and meaninglessness. *Pasada* conveys clearness, brightness, purity of senses, vision, joy, happiness, serenity, and even faith in one's own clear awareness faculty (called *sati* in Pali). It is what keeps *samvega* from turning into despair or depression. Prince Siddhartha experienced *pasada* after watching the serene face of a monk preceded by the sights of a sick man, old man, and dead man and possibly after eating the milk-rice pudding offered by Sujata after six-years of stressful ascetic practice.

I felt *pasada* on many occasions as a child when I had the luminous dream of Buddha around age eleven. It made me less anxious and afraid and feel blessed and safe. I experienced *pasada* also while sitting under the Bodhi Tree for the first time, and on the steps of Lotus Pond at Sarnath near the Deer Park, and while falling asleep recollecting the three refuge names of the Buddha, *Dhamma*, and *Sangha*. My grandma encouraged me to listen to the Pali chanting by monks with respectful, one-pointed concentration. I listened without understanding most words. I feel now, listening to those Pali sound vibrations had some impact on my nonverbal learning. I went into meditative immersion effortlessly just with my conviction in Buddha *dharma*, trust in life, and confidence in myself. So can you!

Wisely attending to whatever makes you alive and happy can bring you in touch with the self-existing natural joy within you that is not dependent on anything external. You can progress in spiritual path without painful striving or ascetic practices by riding on natural joy. You can find joy in the practice of virtue, study of dhamma, beauty in the world, and joy in the happiness of others.

Song of the universe

"Uni" means one and "verse" means song. Remembering many songs of the great poet Rabindranath Tagore (the bard of India, especially the Bengali people) from my teen years, provided much inspiration and energy to continue the practice of aliveness and sublime joy here and now in my own spiritual path. Here is one sample:

Cosmic AWE

In the grand span of time and space
In the vast cosmos, alive with swarming life
At its center I found my place
In wonder, awakens my song!
What makes the world spin and dance
in the up down tides of endless time
Also beats in this very heart of mine
pulsing the stream of blood in my veins
In awe, my song awakens!
Stepping on the meadow by the forest path
A swift fragrance of flowers catches my breath,
The gift of bliss and joy spread all around
In wonder, awakens my song!
Tuning my ears close, opening my eyes wide
Pouring my soul into the earth's bosom,
Within the known
I've searched for the unknown
In awe, my song awakens!

Making space for the sacred in daily life

Sacred is our living connection to the infinite Cosmic womb, the Unified Source Field of cosmic love-light-energy (Tathagatagarbha) that supports all life force and living beings in our planet and the whole universe. Many native and indigenous cultures, ancient myths and sacred texts talk about remembering and nurturing this sacred and intuitive heart connection to keep our mind-body-spirit alive with meaning, purpose, value, freedom and fulfillment.

In your daily or weekly routine create an intentional quiet space for study, contemplation and meditation may be 30 to 45 minute for each day to start to immerse yourself in Dhamma. If breath meditation is difficult initially or at some point start with walking meditation or just sitting silently focusing inward with a candle, crystal, statue, meditation chant or healing sound of nature. Remind yourself to be mindful by coming back to the present with taking three conscious breathing every hour of the day. Notice things just as they are without like and dislike.

Notice how you relate with your own body, your habitual thinking, emotions and attitudes with a sense of care, curiosity and self-compassion. Can you be a little more gentle, kind, heedful and patient today or next ten minutes than yesterday? You may discover gradually that the source of happiness and peace actually lie within your mind. You can develop the power of intention by choosing to let go of anger, blame and fear easily by not clinging to external things, people, validation and conditions. Through radical self-acceptance and self-compassion you become the source of your inner strength, joy and fearless freedom.

A note of caution: Conventional ways of staying busy and alive through parties and group activities, taking the bait of manipulative online marketing, addictive substances of all kinds, materialistic consumerism, and predatory debt-capitalism to make us feel good are not viable long-term organizing principles for a mindful, happy, and healthy society.

The antidote to the modern age of confusion, crisis, dystopia, and cultural insanity is building small sanghas and circles of like-minded spiritual friends around some common cause, mission, vision, and engaged practice together for both personal and social well-being.

"Never doubt that a small group of thoughtful, committed, citizens can change the world"

-Margaret Mead, Anthropologist

CHAPTER 4

Ask

"Ask, and you will receive; seek, and you will find; knock,
and it will be opened to you."
-Matthew 7:7-11

"The art and science of asking questions
is the source of all knowledge."
-Thomas Berger

The process of asking questions or spiritual inquiry is directed by one's own direct experience and wise attention. We can simply begin any inquiry of reality and events at personal or impersonal level by using the words like what, who, when, where, how, and why.

What defines the object of an inquiry, *who* is the subject, *when* and *where* give the time, location, and other details of the context or situation, *how* is the process or plan of getting to a goal or outcome, and *why* takes us to the deeper purpose, intention, and meaning behind the inquiry, action, or intention. Investigating our views, beliefs, opinions, emotions, desires, identities, and defense mechanisms are directly related to our suffering and happiness and are the most important to investigate. We can also do a compassionate inquiry using goodwill and empathy to see the difficult times and challenges and how we overcame some of them using our core strengths, positive inquiry, and kindness.

Some of the sample questions I ask my clients are:

1. What an inspired life goal would be for you to work on for the next seven months?
2. What specifically do you want to accomplish?
3. What would your life look like if you made a commitment today?
4. How would your life change if you start working on this goal?
5. Where are you today in relation to this goal?
6. What have you already accomplished?
7. Who or what event led you to this book page?

Asking the right question at the right time can open the right direction for your dreams and goals in life. It can create the right support and options for your practice and pave the way forward when you do not feel confident and need some expert guidance.

To schedule a complimentary, 30-minute Discovery and Clarity call, visit susmitabarua.com now.
These spots get filled up fast.

Time for deep thinking (contemplation)

I invite you to be present to get the most out of this book. Shut the door, turn off your phone, and get comfy for an hour.

Ponder these reflections and journal your first thoughts.

1. Am I living in an auto-pilot mode or in the driver's seat in my life right now?
2. Why am I making this journey here on earth now?
3. Does life end in death? Either way, how do I live fully with purpose, meaning, and joy?
4. What things are draining my energy, attention, and resources daily?
5. Am I getting kinder and wiser each week with my body-mind-speech?
6. What are three disempowering myths or core beliefs I can see and change now?
7. Who am I? Am I my body? Am I my mind? Who am I not?
8. Who or what can I take with me when I die?
9. Can I stretch 5% out of my comfort zone to become my whole healthy self?
10. What one thing can I let go that will make me and my family happy now?
11. What things am I grateful for now?
12. What is my biggest fear? What if I turn toward my fear and do it anyway?

Let go of worldly preoccupation

A preoccupied mind cannot ask new questions for the mind to open for new discovery. Renunciation is a natural response when there is a sense of violation of one's core living principles and wise nature. The American Trappist monk and social activist, Thomas Merton says it best:

"*The rush and pressure of modern life are a form, perhaps the most common form, of its innate violence. To allow oneself to be carried away by a multitude of conflicting concerns, to surrender to too many demands, to commit oneself to too many projects, to want to help everyone in everything, is to succumb to violence. The frenzy of our activism neutralizes our work for peace. It destroys our own inner capacity for peace. It destroys the fruitfulness of our own work, because it kills the root of inner wisdom which makes work fruitful.*"

Renunciation (*nekhamma*) is the natural wish to be free from all worldly attachments that keep people trapped in the wheel of samsara (repeated suffering). In *buddhadharma*, the right intention of renunciation goes together with good-will and harmlessness. This nourishes wise speech, action, and effort in The Noble Eightfold Path. Buddha declared intention as *kamma* (action). The quality of intention, which arises within the mind as a thought before speech and action, qualifies the fruit (benefit or harm) of the action. Most people are unaware that they are the inheritors of their good and harmful intentions.

What this means to you

It is important to ask yourself what your intention is before you speak on the phone, send that text message or email, or take hasty action on the spur of the moment when things get rough, and emotions are high. Ask yourself, *Am I acting out of ill will or goodwill? How do I want the other person to think, feel, and act toward me? Can I extend the same first?* Knowing your own values and boundaries and stating them clearly helps you detach easily and come to balance and harmony sooner rather than later.

"If by giving up small pleasures, great happiness is to be found, the wise would give up small pleasures, seeing (the prospect of) great happiness."
-Dhammapada, verse 290

Contemplation on death and life

My own deliberate journey inward started with contemplation on life and death. One does not make sense without the other. Yet in our modern culture, school, and work we avoid talking about emotional pain, suffering, grief, death, and divorce close to a pathological level of denial and taboo. Shopping, consumerism, and the material status of success rule our attention, energy, and lives precisely because we are afraid to face the fear of the unknown, even though it is inevitable to all living beings.

According to the Australian author Bronnie Ware, the top five regrets of the dying are:

1. I wish I'd had the courage to live a life true to myself, not the life others expected of me.
2. I wish I hadn't worked so hard.
3. I wish I'd had the courage to express my feelings.
4. I wish I had stayed in touch with my friends.
5. I wish that I had let myself be happier.

Contemplation on life

- Does your life reflect what you truly cherish and value?
- Do you know your heart's true desire?

- What is the vision for your spiritual life?
- What is the vision of your right livelihood?

Case study: In my experience smart immigrant women and highly qualified women of color with Phd in high executive role and sometimes overworked and underpaid jobs have to navigate many inner and outer obstacles at home and work to what they would love to create and experience. With right coaching, simple awareness tools, creative visioning and compassionate listening these women can quickly access their inner voice, vision and intuition and turn around their long-standing stuck situations at work, home and relationship in six to seven months or less.

What is the ancient Arya way of mindful living

*"There are the four traditions of the Noble (Arya)
Ones—original, long-standing, traditional, ancient,
uncorrupted, unadulterated from the beginning—which
are not open to suspicion, will never be open to suspicion,
and are unfaulted by knowledgeable contemplatives
and brahmans. The monks find pleasure and delight
in developing (wholesome mental qualities) and find
pleasure and delight in abandoning (unwholesome mental
qualities). They do not, on account of their pleasure and
delight in developing and abandoning, exalt themselves
or disparage others. In this they are skillful, energetic,
alert, and mindful. This, monks, is said to be a monk
standing firm in the ancient, original traditions
of the Noble Ones."*
-The Ashoka Edict (3rd century BC) and AN 4.28

*The first step of The Noble Tenfold Path begins with
Right View or Full Vision of the path to ultimate peace,*

liberation, and happiness. "And what is 'complete vision' (samma ditthi)? Knowledge with regard to stress, knowledge with regard to the origination of the stress, knowledge with regard to the cessation of stress, knowledge with regard to the path of practice leading to the cessation of stress and ignorance: This is called right view."

-DN 22

What this means for you

You, too, as a conscious leader, mindful professional, social entrepreneur can take pleasure and delight in skillfully developing your mind, body, and speech by cultivating wise habits and abandoning harmful attitudes. I have seen with my clients and students, even a small shift in mindset and mindfulness practice can significantly improve their individual level of happiness, confidence, and resilience to cope with life's inevitable difficulties.

Acinteyya - four imponderables

Some questions cannot be answered. The four imponderables are identified in the Acintita Sutta, AN 4.77, as follows:

1. The Buddha-range of the Buddhas, i.e., the range of powers a Buddha develops as a result of becoming a Buddha
2. The *jhana*-range of one absorbed in *jhana*, i.e., the range of powers that one may obtain while absorbed in *jhana*

3. The precise working out of the results of *kamma* (*karma* in Sanskrit)

4. Speculation about the origin, purpose, etc. of the cosmos is an imponderable that is not to be speculated about (SN 56.41 develops this speculation as the ten indeterminate)

Dhamma vicaya: investigation of *dhamma*

This is the second of seven factors of awakening described by the Buddha. It naturally arises after mindfulness of breath is established. *Vicaya* means to inquire, investigate, and analyze mental objects and states from all angles much like a jeweler inspects the jewel. (The mind is the most precious jewel.)

Abiding thus—ardent, alert, and mindful—one investigates and examines his mental content with wisdom and embarks upon a full inquiry into it. In one who investigates and examines that state with wisdom and embarks upon a full inquiry into it, tireless energy is aroused. In one who has aroused energy, unworldly rapture arises. In one who is rapturous, the body and the mind become tranquil. In one whose body is tranquil and who feels pleasure, the mind becomes concentrated. He closely looks on with equanimity at the mind thus concentrated.

This is how the four foundations of mindfulness (see Chapter 5), developed and cultivated, fulfill the seven enlightenment factors.

CHAPTER 5

Abandon

*"Just as a fallen tree grows back again, if the roots are strong
and unbroken, So suffering sprouts again and again
Until the tendency to crave is not uprooted"*

-Dhammapada 338

"What do you think, Rahula: What is a mirror for?"

"For reflection, sir."

*"In the same way, Rahula, bodily actions, verbal actions, and
mental actions are to be done with repeated reflection."*

-Buddha's sermon to his son Rahula (MN 61)

Abandoning in Buddhist path means abandoning views and habits that cause us and our fellow beings pain and suffering. It is not pushing away difficult people, craving and aversion but gentle letting go of unwholesome and unskillful habits with the recognition of suffering and intention of going forth in spiritual life. Did you know our subconscious mind handles 95% of the processing power in our brain? If we are not aware that our 5% conscious mind has to give instructions and suggestions to the subconscious in clear ways under calm relaxed state, we are just using our old auto-pilot programmed habits. Such habits include unconscious latent tendencies (*anusaya*) and unwholesome mental conditioning and karmic habits (*sankhara*), which are the main cause for confusion, ignorance and repeated suffering. *Anusaya* can be dropped in a moment of insight and intention or more gradually by a process of letting go of that wrong belief, unwholesome view, unskillful intention, and behavior that no longer serve you and harm others.

Abandoning means renouncing and replacing the unwholesome, unskillful, harmful habits with cultivation of the wholesome, skillful, and beneficial habits of body, mind, and speech. This is where you gradually renounce conventional unexamined views of materialistic life and its heedless delusional ways of living, to willingly accept mindful wise view of life, and living with right intention, kind speech, right action, livelihood, effort and meditation as laid out in the Noble Eightfold Path of the ancient ones for the benefit of all beings and the planet.

We all have an intuitive sense of what is not working, where our cravings lead us to bad health, carelessness, and obsessions. Bad habits, like weeds, take over a garden if not properly attended to for weeks, months, or years. With awareness and intention, you can start them pulling gently or energetically as the job requires. This process needs to be done with loving awareness and not anger or resentment toward yourself or others. Unskillful habits like biting your nails, checking your cell phone while visiting a friend, not finishing a sentence or task before moving to the next one, drains your energy, attention, and self-confidence and aggravate others.

What this means to you as a woman or man, that you clearly see that you are not your habit or behavior. There are often internal and external causes and conditions that lead you to pick up certain habits while growing up, sometimes to survive unpleasant people or situations. Sustaining the habit of denial or avoidance of difficult conversation keeps us stuck in our pain and victimhood. You can see the pattern as a pattern and not identify it as "I, me, mine, or myself" and then take simple steps to disrupt it.

> "The essence of strategy is choosing what not to do."
> -Michael Porter

Make an intention for a new habit with empowering new thoughts and words. Take a ten-minute pause, meditate on it, and repeat the pause before taking the next drink, drug, or cigarette. See videos on the long-term impact, pain, and cost of this habit on your own health, happiness, relationship, children, and bank account. Find or make a support group of people who are committed to quit and who did so successfully. Stop listening to the inner critic pointing to past failures.

You may choose to intentionally practice one of the five ethical trainings or one of ten virtues (paramitas) a week for five to fifteen weeks to develop a wholesome mental state free from hindrances. Setting daily practice of meditation also helps cultivation of wholesome states, which is required to sustain mindfulness at work.

The list of five Buddhist ethics (panca sila) are voluntary commitments to abstain from

1. Killing living beings
2. Taking what is not given
3. Sexual misconduct
4. Lying deliberately
5. Taking intoxicants that make one heedless

Imagine what would happen if every child, citizen, law enforcement, and public official took this ethical training in a democracy. *Sila* promotes universal respect for life, safety, trust, awareness, social responsibility, harmony, happiness, health, good karma, pure mind, true wealth, and success. Most importantly, it also prepares the mind for mindful meditation and calm unification of mind in *samadhi*.

The list of ten virtues, which is widely promoted in Buddhadharma, are the *pāramitās* (perfections): *dāna* (generosity), *sīla* (ethical conduct), *nekkhamma* (renunciation), *paññā* (wisdom), *viriya* (energy), *khanti* (patience), *sacca* (honesty), *adhiṭṭhāna* (determination), *mettā* (goodwill), and *upekkhā* (equanimity).

Transforming *tanha* to *chanda*

Craving (*tanha*): The thirst or desire for some pleasant sensual object can turn into strong feelings (*vedana*) of craving (tanha), clinging, and grasping (*upadana*) leading to becoming/existence (bhava) and birth/rebirth (*jati*) in different realms. *Tanha* usually manifests as reactive tension, stress, negative emotional loops, and narratives in the mind. Aversion is the other side of craving. It is a strong feeling (*vedana*) of dislike, animosity, hate, and revulsion for unpleasant things or people. Both craving and aversion are conditioned reactions to perceived gain, stress, fear, pain, and loss. Both these emotions have an unnatural, neurotic, obsessive, and unhealthy nature to them. Throughout the day, our minds are run by the push and pull of like, dislike, or neutral feelings (*vedana*). The neutral feeling tones lead to boredom, indifference, apathy, and ignorance. Numbing, suppressing, or denial of unpleasant feeling tone is not conducive to spiritual growth. Bring openness, kindness, curiosity, inquiry, and gentle letting go to difficult and unpleasant emotions.

> There is no fire like lust, no grasping like hate
> No snare like delusion, no river like craving
> -Dhammapada (ch 18:151)

The delusion (*moha*) of self and self-attachment runs our lives. It's a profound and primordial dissatisfaction, neediness, a painful feeling that something is missing, of being bereft, lonely, and cut off. It's just there, all the time, in the bones of our being. The root of all this is ignorance or lack of awareness. Attachment to views, likes, and dislikes are constantly pulling or pushing us away from relaxing into the present moment experience.

Chanda usually arises from a wholesome mind state of love and acceptance. It is a wholesome desire as an eagerness to offer, to commit, to apply oneself to meditation (*ajahn sucitto*), Buddha spoke of two kinds of desire: desire that arises from ignorance and delusion which is called *tanhā*—craving—and desire that arises from wisdom and intelligence, which is called *kusala-chanda*, or *dhamma-chanda*, or more simply, *chanda* (*ajahn jayasaro*). In my view, there is a third meaning of *chanda* as the rhythm of the universe (like *Rta* in Veda). *Chanda* implies desire that is in harmony with the natural rhythm of seasons, sun, moon, and life cycles, and our own body-mind rhythms of breath, heartbeat, vagus nerve, sleep cycles, hormones, and circadian rhythm.

What this means to you

Be aware and mindful of your strong likes and dislikes, jealousy, anger, lack, and fear. If you are unconscious of your pattern of attachment and aversion, you can harm your own well-being, mental health, and peace, and those around you. The good news is that Buddha found a way to end craving and aversion. The way out is The Noble Eightfold Path (Tenfold with outcome).

The Buddha talked about five types of habitual cravings that keep us locked to the wheel of *samsara*, *dukkha*, and pull the undisciplined body-mind in six directions of pleasure (away from unpleasant pain) like six wild animals. They are:

1. Craving for sensual pleasure (*kama-taṇhā*) driven by six senses
2. Craving for existence or becoming (*bhava-taṇhā*)
3. Craving for nonexistence (*vibhava-taṇhā*)
4. Clinging to wrong views (*miccha ditthi*), especially wrong views and view of a substantial self (*sakkaya-ditthi*)
5. Clinging to rites and rituals, thinking they will liberate or enlighten you. It is dangerous to follow a leader or teacher teaching wrong views.

There are seven ways of abandoning mental taints (*asavas*) and defilements of sensual grasping, becoming, and delusion.

> "Monks, the ending of the fermentations is for one who knows and sees, I tell you, not for one who does not know and does not see. For one who knows what and sees what? Appropriate attention and inappropriate attention. When a monk attends inappropriately, unarisen fermentations arise, and arisen fermentations increase. When a monk attends appropriately, unarisen fermentations do not arise, and arisen fermentations are abandoned. There are fermentations to be abandoned by seeing, those to be abandoned by restraining, those to be abandoned by using, those to be abandoned by tolerating, those to be abandoned by avoiding, those to be abandoned by dispelling, and those to be abandoned by developing."
>
> -Sabbasava Sutta, MN2

What this means for you

To tame the six wild untamed senses of the body-mind, first establish mindfulness of the body. Bring your attention and focus inward to your breath and body sensation for one to three minutes every hour. This will give you a sense of inner calm, ease, and peace to find relief amid daily stress and overwhelm. Daily stress and anxiety can paralyze your prefrontal cortex, the brain's executive function, such as judgment, focus, and planning.

As a result, addicted persons lose the ability to be reflective (regulate behavior), and impulses take a stronger hold over their motivations and behaviors. Addicts need to be aware of certain stressful situations (like getting too hungry, angry, lonely, or tired) so they can resist the temptation to consume. Freedom from wanting and craving mind is true freedom in *buddhadharma*. What triggers your emotional stress reactions?

Out of our obsessive craving for existence comes many other cravings, craving for survival, reproduction, security, comfort, success, power, affection, recognition, certainty, wealth, and so forth. Craving for non-existence is the craving not to experience painful perception, situations, and unpleasant people in the current or future life. This sort of craving may include attempts at self-annihilation, suicide, or mass murder, mass shootings, and war. White males accounted for 69.7% of suicide deaths in 2020, and firearms accounted for 52.8% of all suicide deaths in the US.

What this means for you

Discover and develop your own middle way of living a balanced life of harmony with moderation, self-care, and non-attachment, renouncing extreme views of self-indulgence or self-denial, and eternalism or annihilationism. Cultivate a kind heart, open mind, and a wholesome growth mindset.

Ignorance of the Law of Causation (*paṭiccasamuppāda*)

In his profound teaching on the Law of Causation, known as the Dependent Origination, all the arising and passing cycles of mind-body impulses, sensations, thoughts, feelings, perceptions, intentions, actions in consciousness from beginningless time is taking place on the foundation of ignorance, i.e., not seeing impermanence, not recognizing *dukkha*, and not understanding not-self (insubstantial) nature of all existential experience. This misperception happens, not just in individual consciousness, but at the level of collective thinking and systems level as in racism, sexism, and capitalism. All things are interdependent and arise in dependence on other things, causes and conditions.

When this is, that is.

With the arising of this, that arises.

When this is not, neither is that.

With the cessation of this, that ceases.

Human mind gets entangled and polluted through proliferation of mental concepts, ideas, and extreme fetter of views creating a net of delusional perception and thinking called *papanca*, which drives social quarrels and strife (Honeyball Sutta MN 18). In modern days, we may see *papanca* in our political, financial, legal, and work arenas and within political-social networks and family group dysfunctions.

From *ayoniso* to *yoniso manasikara*

Making the intention of turning away from unwise (*ayoniso*) to wise source (*yoniso*) attention in daily life is very impactful in the long run. One of the primary ways to incline our life and mind from habitual reactivity and suffering to responsibility, meaning, happiness, freedom, and peace is by recognizing and abandoning *ayoniso* (uwise) to *yoniso manasikara* (wise attention to the source, causes or origins of things). Buddha's become enlightened through wisely attending things with *yoniso manasikara*. The word *yoni* refers to the womb, matrix, source, or place of origin.

Yonisomanasikara conveys a sense of thoroughly, wisely, and penetratively attending or investigating something with loving awareness down to its underlying causes and conditions. It is one of the four factors of stream-entry (*sotapanna*) and the intention of this book. It is the first stage of awakening in the four-stage map described by the Buddha. Three of the ten fetters that bind us to *samsara* are broken and the *dhamma chakkhu* (eye of *dhamma*) is opened. Goals are externally driven and outcome oriented, but intentions come from inside from choosing a holistic view and wise direction of life that is in alignment with one's deepest values, vision, and purpose. Another way to see wholesome intention is to see body, mind, emotions, and spirit as fully aligned.

'Seeing danger in what's not dangerous
And not seeing danger in what is,
Those who take up wrong views go to bad rebirth.

Finding fault in what's not at fault
And seeing no fault in what is,
Those who take up wrong views
Go to a bad rebirth

But knowing fault as fault,
And the faultless, as the faultless
Those who take up the right views
Go to good rebirth.

-Dhammapada 327-329

Someone faced with a difficult illness, pain, or death gets intensely focused for healing the disease to be alive and healthy. In a similar way, *yonisomanasikara* inclines one's mind and practice toward ultimate liberation and awakening (*nibbana*) from the prison or matrix of *papanca* or mental proliferation. With *yonisomanasikara*, thoughts and motivations are intentionally inclined toward wholesome direction by abandoning unwholesome negative thinking and harmful conduct based on sensual desire, ill will, and delusion. Five hindrances to mindfulness are nourished through unwise attention and *seven factors of awakening* are fed by wise attention. Discernment of these two kinds of attention is vital for awakening.

Buddha describes the benefit and power of first stage awakening as *sotapanna* (stream entry). The stream is The Noble Eightfold (Tenfold with outcomes) path. This has been forgotten or downplayed in comparison to Arahants and Bodhisattvas even among Buddhists. A *sotapanna* has permanently stopped falling into lower realm rebirths (in animal, asura, hungry ghost, and hell realms), gained unshakable confidence in Buddha, *dharma*, and *sangha*, opened the intuitive eye (*dhamma chakkhu*) of the true *dhamma*, and broken three chains of skeptical doubt (*vicikiccha*), self-view (*sakkaya ditthi*), and belief vows and rituals (*silabbata*). They gained the wisdom of wholesome view (*samma ditthi*) and are bound for full awakening in this life or at most seven lifetimes in human or god (divine) realms. For modern day contemplatives and seekers of any Buddhist tradition 'stream-entry' is the doorway to enter the true dhamma of the ancient noble ones that leads to Nibbana, the highest happiness, peace and freedom. Buddha described *sotapanna* or stream-winner as:

Sole dominion over the earth,
going to heaven,
lordship over all worlds:
the fruit of stream-entry
Surpasses them all.
-Dhammapada 178

The Buddha also spoke of the importance of having wise people of integrity as friends, companions, and colleagues (*kalyanamitta*) and having such friends is not just a part but the whole of the spiritual life.

What this means to you

Time and attention diverted by digital products, social media, consumer ads, political news, or difficult people must be reclaimed with right effort. Habitual dwelling on past hurts or future worries and clinging to self-view is a common cause for stress, anxiety, and depression, especially among youth and young adults. Our thoughts and emotions can be very addictive, just like drugs or alcohol. Cognitive rigidity and rumination do not lead to new possibilities or solutions now or in future.

As Buddha said, "all that we are is the result of what we thought." Write down five to ten disempowering thoughts and core beliefs you hold now and change them to simple positive empowering statements. Record it to listen or read twice every day for a week or until they feel natural to you. Abandoning unskillful habits of thought, speech, and action begins with the intention to change *ayoniso* to *yoniso manasikara*. You can change your mindset a little at a time. See how it affects your level of confidence and happiness.

"The deathless (*nibbana*) can be attained even today by those who thoroughly apply themselves," proclaims a verse in ancient psalms of enlightened nuns (Therigatha 513). It takes one upstream to the source or knowledge of ending suffering and ignorance rather than downstream to delusional mass consciousness. The Buddhist path is called 'going against the stream' of habitual craving, anger, and ignorance.

In my own experience, the wise attention (*yoniso manasikara*) was also accompanied and supported by two other states of consciousness that are inherent in all human children: 1) the beginner's mind, and 2) basic goodness. When I was ten years old and visited Bodh-Gaya, Rajgir, and Sarnath for the first time, I witnessed the playfulness of children—both poor street children and young and old Tibetan lamas clad in red robes.

I had this inquiry, *Why do human children born with basic goodness grow up to be such sad and unhappy adults?"* I had no doubt that our fundamental human nature is basically good. Also, I would spend hours watching the stars, filled with wonder and awe. I knew that the adult world was very survival oriented, far removed from the magical world of a child where anything is possible.

You, too, can trust your beginner's mind experiences, intuition of your own heart-mind, and incline it toward developing your own path to ending ignorance and suffering. The Buddha said: "This mind, monks, is luminous but defiled by visiting defile-ments. The uninstructed person does not understand as it is."

What this means to you is, you can learn to sit with your feelings of anger and pain (*vedana*) and inquire into their causes and conditions so you can relate and respond with kindness rather than anger or hate, creating more pain. The human mind has the capacity to transcend all fear and limitation and reach its pure, luminous, non-clinging, and knowing awake nature.

From *pamada* to *appamada*

The Pali word "*pamada*" means mad, intoxicated, drunk, deluded, heedless, unrestrained, and clouded. The cost of drug addiction (tobacco, alcohol, and illegal and prescription drugs) to society in the US exceeds $800 billion dollars. There are many other kinds of addiction beside drugs, and all have a compulsive craving element to them. Our negative thoughts and emotions can become addictive and delusional and mindful-awareness is used to interrupt and change these patterns. The third of the five educational training (called precepts) for the mind is to abstain from taking intoxicants because they cause heedlessness and are detrimental to mental sanity and physical health and cause great harm to self, family, and community. The opposite of craving is aversion (resenting, not wanting and avoiding what is present) for unpleasant things. Both create internal conflict and suffering.

In ordinary conventional life of the uninformed, uninstructed (*puthujjana*) in dharma and karma of moral causation, *pamada* is common. And "*appamada*" means cultivating heedfulness and clarity of mind, diligently with sanity. *Appamada* is the way of life for Ariya, meaning a noble person who is living mindfully and has attained direct insight into the truth of reality and *dhamma*. The whole Buddhist path is to transform the human mental condition from heed-less state of *pamada* to whole-hearted mindful state of *appamada*.

A person of *pamada* is harmful to self and others and failing in human duty to self and society. In the Appamada Sutta (SN 3.7), King Pasenadi Kosala said to Buddha, the Blessed One: "Is there, Lord, any one quality that keeps both kinds of benefit secure—benefits in this life and benefits in lives to come?" Buddha responded, "Diligent heedfulness, great king. Heedfulness is the one quality that keeps both kinds of benefits secure—benefits in this life and benefits in lives to come."

What this means for you is, even if you do not believe in past and future lives, since life is short and finite for everyone, it serves you best to associate with and listen to wise friends (*kalyanamitta*). It could be your parents, spouse, friends, mentors, and your own inner voice of guidance. Association with wise friends is one of four factors in the first stage of awakening (*sotapanna*).

> "Vaya Dhamma Sankhara Appamadena Sampadetha
> means - 'All conditioned things are impermanent.
> Work for your liberation with appamada."
> -Last words of the Buddha

> "Monks, I know of no other single thing of such power to
> cause the arising of wholesome states, if not yet arisen,
> or to cause the waning of unwholesome states,
> if already arisen, as appamāda."
> -Buddha (AN 1.6)

From form to formless and *sunyata*

The best way to ground our body-mind is to connect with heaven and earth, using our body as the conduit of energy between the two. My favorite object of meditation is resting in the empty space of clear blue sky, a habit I developed while taking afternoon naps in my no-school days. In the Cula Sunyata Sutta, the Buddha encouraged his disciples to meditate on emptiness:

"Monks, here (in empty space) there is no stress due to the defilements of sensuality, desire to be reborn, or ignorance. There is only this modicum of stress, namely that associated with the six sense fields dependent on this body and conditioned by life. ...whatever ascetics and brahmins enter and remain in the pure, ultimate, supreme *sunyata* —whether in the past, future, or present—all of them enter and remain in this same pure, ultimate, supreme emptiness.

"So, Ānanda, you should train like this: 'We will enter and remain in the pure, ultimate, supreme emptiness.' That is how you should train."

> Wisdom arises from (spiritual) practice
> Without practice it decays.
> Knowing this two way path for gain and loss
> Conduct yourself, so that wisdom grows.
>
> -Dh 20:282

Whoever having given up human bondage,
Has gone beyond heavenly bondage,
Is unbound from all bondage,
I call a brahmin.

An arahant, whose destination is not known

By gods, gandhabbas, and humans,
Whose toxins are extinct,
I call a brahmin.

-Dhammapada 26:417;420

In his teachings the Buddha spoke of showing respect to people who are upright and apply themselves to master the discipline of the true dhamma. For the people who show respect for the worthy and noble ones, four things increase: lifespan, beauty, happiness and strength.

CHAPTER 6

Accept

To offer no resistance to life is to be in a state of grace, ease, and lightness.
-Ekhart Tolle

The moment you accept the troubles you've been given, doors open.
-Rumi

After recognition of suffering and its causes, the first two steps of the Four Noble Truths, acceptance is a key transformational point in moving forward in your spiritual growth and outlook expansion. It is preceded by a willingness to let go of the past hurts, renounce old habits, and give up expectations for things to be different than what they are now. It is a soft and gentle opening of the heart to greater life after it has been wounded and closed for many months or years. Complete acceptance of yourself for the sake of inner peace becomes the complete acceptance of everyone else. It opens the heart to receive the generosity, abundance, and goodness of nature and all beings, to be grateful for things and people to whom we are connected, to forgive others, and to trust the regularity of *dhamma* and the principle of *kamma* already operating in life and the cosmos.

It is letting go of the resistance to change, dropping the burden of old unpleasant memories, allowing a space for self-care, for a new possibility and hope to emerge from within. One can finally relax and experience some sense of calm, serenity, and inner peace. Acceptance also leads to the expansion of your heart's capacity for unbounded love and a willingness to go deeper in your mindful inquiry process and meditation practice.

What this means to you is to let things just be, accepting things and people as they are because we cannot change other people, we can only change how we react and respond to them. Here is a story of deep acceptance and letting go.

A woman named Nima had a difficult relationship with her mother in-law, who had complex attachment and trauma issues with her son. This was affecting Nima's own relationship with her spouse right after their marriage. After four years of trying to please her, Nima gave up the possibility of ever making her mother in-law happy. With mindfulness and *metta* meditation, she began to silently send love (*metta*) to her mother-in-law in another country far away. This *metta* practice helped Nima to not only clear all resentment and painful memories but find the spaciousness to be truly free inside. When she visited her mother in-law seven years later, Nima only took her mother in-law's cold anxious hand in hers and her mother in-law would not let that go for a very long time. There was just a silent exchange of warm compassion and gratitude.

"Your relationships improve drastically and the tension in your mind decreases significantly when you can simply accept people for who they are, instead of fixating on how they should change to be more like you."

-Yung Pueblo, Clarity and Connection.

Unwholesome to wholesome states

My own entry to the first two steps, namely the Right or Wholesome View and Wholesome Intention of The Noble Eightfold (or Tenfold with outcome) Path was based on abandoning the unwholesome and accepting the wholesome mental state (in thoughts, feelings, perception, volitional habits, and consciousness) as the natural state of mind.

Venerable Sariputta identified the following sixteen cases (*pariyaya*) through which a noble disciple could achieve right view:

- The unwholesome and the wholesome
- Nutriments
- The Four Noble Truths (discussed as one case)
- The Twelve Causes (Nidana Sutta) of Dependent Origination (discussed as twelve individual cases)
- The Taints

(See Sammaditthi Sutta, Bhikkhu Nanamoli and Bhikkhu Bodhi 1994, MN-9 accesstoinsight.org)

> "Bhikkhus, just as the dawn is the forerunner and first indication of the rising of the sun, so is right view the forerunner and first indication of wholesome states. For one of right view, bhikkhus, right intention springs up. For one of right intention, right speech springs up. For

*one of right speech, right action springs up. For one
of right action, right livelihood springs up. For one of
right livelihood, right effort springs up. For one of right
effort, right mindfulness springs up. For one of right
mindfulness, right concentration springs up. For one of
right concentration, right knowledge springs up. For one
of right knowledge, right deliverance springs up."*
-Anguttara Nikaya 10:121

I could clearly see the repeated thought pattern of reactive-ness against others' hurtful speech and actions toward me, making them permanent and clinging to them as me, mine, or I. At the time I did not have the mindfulness skill to process strong emotions, nor the skill of Right Speech needed to be both vulnerable and assertive. This left me feeling powerless in situations of inequality, exclusion, and power imbalance. The first thing I was able to do to stop my wildly swinging mind was to unplug from past hurts and future worries with the power of wise attention and intention and sustain that with the wholesome mental state of *metta* in the present.

In the Ariyan Dhamma, the practice of meditation unfolds from start to finish as a process of mental cleansing. The process begins with the recognition of the dangers in unwholesome states: they are real corruptions of our being that need to be restrained and eliminated. The consumma-tion is reached in the gradual replacement of the defilements through the cultivation of their wholesome antidotes (like aversion replaced with loving-kindness and clinging with detachment and letting go) and stilling of mental fabri-cations with wholesome mindfulness (*sati* and *samadhi*). "One does not tolerate an arisen unwholesome thought (*like anger, envy, pride*), one abandons it, dispels it, abolishes it, and nullifies it" (MN 2).

The most surprising thing for me was to recognize how long I carried the hurt and resentment without feeling safe to express it. That is how my mind was conditioned in my Indian culture. I was desperately looking for a way to release the addictive negative emotional loops going on in my brain like a broken record again and again. A little card with the "Serenity Prayer" caught my attention. I kept repeating the prayer like a mantra for two weeks, as it made perfect sense to me at the time both for my rational and intuitive side. It taught me how to draw emotional boundaries and protect my serenity and develop my courage and wisdom.

"Give me the *serenity* to accept the things I cannot change (other people and situations)
The *courage* to change the things I can (my mental state, and choices)
And the *wisdom* (*discernment*) to know the difference between the two."

What this means to you is, when you meet a challenging situation or difficult person, you can always stop and visualize, taking a pause and not reacting internally or externally. While clearly observing your thoughts and emotions without judgements in your sitting meditation, you may see your suffering is not as much due to what the other person said or did, but due to clinging to your own reactive thoughts and emotions around it for hours, days, or months after the event took place.

Buddha called this habit of repeated self-affliction as the second arrow. We suffer by internalizing our habitual defenses of fight, flight, freeze, and fawn (pleasing others) tendencies. We cannot always avoid painful interactions, but we can limit suffering by letting go of the anger, resentment, anxiety, and pain by stopping the second arrow of self-affliction and habitual tendencies on the spot, or within a short time with wise attention and intention.

Using the power of intention (*samma sankappa*) and the "Serenity Prayer," I was able to completely change my *kleshas* and self-afflictive emotional pathways in three to four weeks. *Kleshas*, in Buddhism, are mental states (driven by ignorance, attachment, and aversion) that cloud the mind and manifest in unskillful thoughts, speech, and actions. The serenity prayer also helped me naturally ease into the mindfulness practice of serenity and insight.

It was a huge relief that I did not need to change or correct others and only needed to work on my fear of change and conflict with courage and compassion. I recommend using any meaningful chant, prayer or quote to clean out any negativity in your mind. Some great universal vedic prayers from India are "*Asato ma Sadgamaya*" from Brhadaranyaka Upanishad and the Gayatri mantra, "*Om bhur bhuva swaha*," from Rigveda. I feel listening to the Pali chants with one-pointed attention also helps raise your overall vibration and comprehension (non-verbal) of the *dhamma*.

Healing with four divine emotions

Healing the heart is a very necessary first step for making progress in mindful meditation. Buddha taught the four *brahmaviharas* (divine abodes), also called the four immeasurable states, to both heal and open the heart so our mind can be unbounded and released from the five hindrances.

Buddhist teacher Gil Fronsdal calls it the four faces of love of the Brahma (a creator God, in Hindu myth). Each face of the wise heart —universal friendliness (*metta*), compassion (*karuna*), appreciative joy (*mudita*), and equanimity (*upekkha*)—can be developed and directed to specific people in our lives now to heal and improve our inner relationships. With these emotions we can build our inner strength, confidence, safety, resilience, and courage; go beyond survival fear and anxiety and stop craving for external attention, pleasure, and validation. Friendliness is the antidote for animosity or hate, compassion is the antidote for cruelty or cold indifference, appreciative joy is the antidote for jealousy or disparagement, and equanimity is the antidote for agitation and anxiety.

Buddhist ethics: the ends do not justify the means

The primary factor contributing to your happiness is your own ethical and skillful action. It means doing no harm, taking full responsibility (ownership and accountability) of your unskillful habits, intentional actions (*kamma*), privilege, and power to create and influence reality in beneficial ways. All of life is interdependent and connected at the deepest level of life energy and consciousness. Harming, oppressing, and killing another living being intentionally is equivalent to harming one's own life and potential for total liberation. One can verify the truth of *dhamma* and *kamma* with a strong desire to gain release from suffering inherent in all conditioned existence with the first glimpse of awakening (*nibbana*) called stream-entry (*sotapanna*).

The karmic consequence of using intentional violence with body, mind and speech is heavy. That is why mindfulness must be based on the foundation of ethics, if we desire true safety without fear, happiness, peace and freedom.

> All tremble at violence
> All fear death
> Life is dear to all
> Seeing other living beings as yourself
> Do not kill or cause others to kill.
>
> Whoever uses violence to harm
> The nonviolent and innocent
> Quickly goes to one of ten conditions:
> Intense pain or great loss
> Bodily injury or insanity
> Serious illness or vicious slander
> Oppression from rulers or loss of relatives
> Home consumed by fire or wealth destroyed
> With the breakup of the body
> The foolish one falls to hell.
> -Dhammapada 10:129;137-140

Buddhas are only educators and guides showing the way to emancipation, each person must make the effort to enter the path and walk till awakening or nibbana. Once, a deva (divine being) came down following the advice of *Saka* (the King of devas) to get the answer to his question from Buddha himself. The *deva* respectfully asked, "Please teach us what the highest blessings for divine and human beings are." Buddha gave this list of thirty-eight blessings in the Mahamangala Sutta.

Life's great blessings (Mahamangala Sutta)

Remembering and counting your blessings regularly incline your mind toward goodwill, gratitude, and wise attention. It also expands the whole-hearted vision and intentions for mindful living and a holy life.

Not to associate with fools, to associate with the wise, and honor those who are worthy of honor;

This is the Blessing Supreme.

To live in a suitable locality, to have done meritorious actions in the past, and to have set oneself on the right course (toward emancipation); this is Blessing Supreme.

Vast-learning, perfect handicraft a highly trained discipline and a pleasant speech; this is Blessing Supreme.

The support of father and mother, the cherishing of wife and children and peaceful occupations, this is the Blessing Supreme.

Liberal giving, righteous conduct, the helping of relatives and blameless actions; this is the Blessing Supreme.

To cease and abstain from evil, forbearance with respect to intoxicants and steadfastness in virtue; this is Blessing Supreme.

Reverence, humility, contentment, bearing gratitude and opportune hearing of the Dhamma; this is Blessing Supreme.

Patience, being easy to advise, sight of the Samanas (holy men), and timely discussion of the Dhamma; this is Blessing Supreme.

Self-control, living a noble life, realizing the Noble Truths and the attainment of Nibbāna; this is Blessing Supreme.

He whose mind does not waver, by contact with worldly contingencies, sorrowless, stainless and secure;
this is Blessing Supreme.

To them, fulfilling matters such as these, everywhere invincible,
In every way secure; these are Blessings Supreme."

-(SN 2.4)

Action alone cannot undo the effect of negative feeling and disempowering thoughts of blame, cynicism, and ill will. Our goodwill and intentions for the planet and humanity can become like a sustained meditation and prayer. The ancient Jewish sect called Essene describes the power of prayer to move beyond any physical limits when our emotions, thoughts and feelings in body-mind are perfectly aligned (Gregg Braden, *Inner Technology of Prayer*, 2011).

What this *sutta* means to you is that you can follow the main markers or goals of a truly happy spiritual life where you do not have to figure out things on your own. Many people have remorse and regret for the time, attention, energy, and wealth not given to their children, spouse, parents, or people they loved or their own passion or dream to pursue different interests or causes they deeply care about. Keeping priorities and balance in work-life-relationships is the hardest thing in the stressful attention-deficit modern culture. Write down your vision for a mindful life and work and share it with a trusted partner or spiritual friend to keep you motivated on the path.

Embracing our human emotional journey

As human beings, we are emotional by nature. Yet we often avoid feeling our unpleasant emotions and cling to pleasant feelings. This human bypassing of the emotional journey creates more stress and sickness, not just in our personal body-mind, but in social psychology, collective mind, health, and well-being. We also identify with our emotions as belonging to me, mine, or myself. We rarely see them with neutral awareness, nor investigate the causes and conditions leading to certain habitual or conditioned patterns of thoughts and emotions. Suffering comes from resisting life in the present moment.

This lack of recognition, suppression, and denial of habitual emotions (like anger, resentment, despair, grief, envy, guilt, shame, and blame) keep us emotionally ignorant and unintelligent. It causes much pain and unnecessary suffering with home, work, and community relationships. We have all experienced uncaring, narcissistic friends, partners, and leaders with no regard for development of empathy and compassion. The third foundation of mindful awareness (mind on mind) is to notice our thoughts and emotions (mental phenomena) and how their nature (positive or reactive) affects our moods and mental states.

Change in life is inevitable, and change is an emotional journey. Emotional awareness, empathy, and mastery is vitally important for both personal and collective psychological and spiritual growth of humanity at this time. Our self-view and self-image are very much shaped by our social-cultural-race-gender identity, role, and status and all are conditioned by cultural meanings, stereotypes, perceptions, and social group expectations.

According to the young poet and meditator, Diego Perez (Yung Pueblo pen name), the six signs of maturity are:

- being open to vulnerability, learning and letting go
- seeing more perspectives than just your own
- accepting responsibility for your happiness
- prioritizing practices that help you grow
- pausing to think instead of reacting
- honesty with yourself and others.

Map of Human Emotion, Psychological and Spiritual Growth

The image, next page, adapted from the book *Power vs. Force* by Dr. David R. Hawkins, maps the relationship between the human state of consciousness (or feeling state as calibrated by kinesiology or muscle testing) and human behavior. Awakening and enlightened state of consciousness calibrates from level 700 to 1,000 in this logarithmic scale.

He saw feeling as more primary than thought. Letting go involves being aware of a feeling, letting it come up, staying with it, and letting it run its course without wanting to make it different or do anything about it. Then, the energy of the feeling rises to a higher level.

We have been conditioned to think that force is power, that to control the behavior of others we need to apply external physical and mental force (which may work in the short run in the material 3D realm) but fails in the higher invisible dimension of consciousness and energy.

True power comes from the unbounded realm of spirit and love beyond ego and is attained through personal mental development, deep contemplation, and mindful spiritual practices. The map below is a useful guide to see where you are in the consciousness scale and how you can develop wholesome mental states. All negative emotions that cause suffering lie below the level of 200 or courage.

MAP OF CONSCIOUSNESS by David R. Hawkins
(image credit from Kimberly Fosu, got it online)

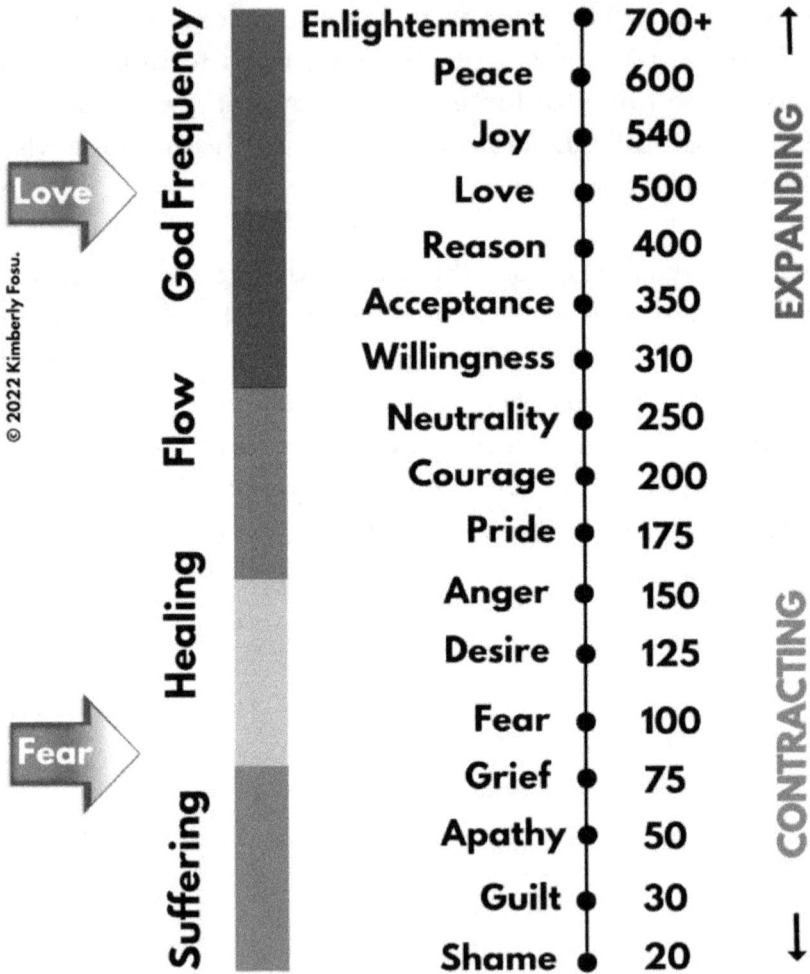

It takes vulnerability, courage, and willingness to examine our hidden beliefs, shadow side, biases, maladaptive defenses, repressed emotions, and traumas. The book *The Body Keeps*

the Score by Bessel van der Kolk eloquently articulates how trauma and overwhelming experiences affect the development of brain, mind, and body awareness, all of which are closely intertwined. The resulting derailments have a profound impact on the capacity for love and work. The energy of the trauma is stored in our bodies' tissues (mostly muscles and fascia) until it can be released. This stored trauma typically leads to pain and progressively erodes a body's health. Emotions are the vehicles the body relies on to transform energy to find balance after a trauma.

According to Bhikkhu Bodhi, the Buddha points to two internal heart-mind qualities as the underlying safeguards of ethics. They act as the protectors of both the individual and society as a whole. These two qualities are called *hiri* and *ottappa* in Pali. *Hiri* is an innate sense of shame over moral transgression; *ottappa* is moral dread, fear of the consequences of wrongdoing. The Buddha calls these two states the bright guardians of the world *(sukha lokapala)*. By cultivating within ourselves the qualities of moral shame and fear of wrongdoing we not only accelerate our own progress along the path to deliverance, serve as ethical etc. protectors and guardians of the world.

CHAPTER 7

Aware

"Awareness is the greatest agent for change."
-Eckhart Tolle

"One who looks outside, dreams. One who looks inside, awakens."
-Carl Jung

The Buddhist practice of mindful-awareness (sati) is all about transforming our mental states from its habitual stress, anxiety, and reactivity to its natural relaxed, calm, content, and wholesome state. As children, we may have experienced moments of this wholesome undisturbed state of no lack and no limit at certain times. There are many subtle aspects of mindful-awareness that cannot all be captured in a definition. To develop unshakable stability and peace of mind, to overcome all sorrow, pain, lamentation, grief, and suffering the Buddha gave his teachings on four establishments of mindfulness (Satipatthana Sutta, MN 10) and four types of meditative immersion (Samadhi Sutta AN 4.41).

The meditation instructions given by the Buddha are found in two main discourses: the first one done in mostly sitting posture is called mindful awareness practice of natural breathing

(Anapanasati sutta MN 118) in the form of a tetrad (group of four). The second discourse (Satipatthana sutta MN10 and DN 22) is on establishing awareness in the four domains of 1) body, 2) feelings, 3) mind, and 4) the principles of dhamma. They are called four establishments or four foundations of mindfulness for sustaining and deepening meditative awareness throughout the day in all four body positions (sitting, walking, standing and lying). Anapanasati leads to Satipatthana, and Satipatthana includes Anapana. Together they help to calm, unify, purify and develop the mind for wholesome concentration (samma samadhi), and deep wisdom.

> "Mindfulness of in and out breathing, when developed
> and pursued, bears great fruit of great benefit.
> Mindfulness of in and out breathing, when developed and
> pursued, brings the four establishments of mindfulness
> to their culmination. The four foundations of mindfulness,
> when developed and pursued, bring the seven factors
> for awakening to their culmination. The seven factors for
> awakening, when developed and pursued, bring clear
> knowing and liberation to their culmination."
> -Buddha, MN 118

Satipaṭṭhāna	Ānāpānasati	Tetrads
1. Contemplation of the body	1. Breathing long (Knowing Breath)	First Tetrad
	2. Breathing short (Knowing Breath)	
	3. Experiencing the whole body	
	4. Tranquillising the bodily activities	
2. Contemplation of feelings	5. Experiencing rapture	Second Tetrad
	6. Experiencing bliss	
	7. Experiencing mental activities	
	8. Tranquillising mental activities	
3. Contemplation of the mind	9. Experiencing the mind	Third Tetrad
	10. Gladdening the mind	
	11. Centering the mind in samadhi	
	12. Releasing the mind	
4. Contemplation of Dhammas	13. Contemplating impermanence	Fourth Tetrad
	14. Contemplating fading of lust	
	15. Contemplating cessation	
	16. Contemplating relinquishment	

Mindful meditation (*samma-sati* and *samadhi*)

With the influx of internet, social-media, technology, and mobile phones constantly hooking our attention, learning how to foster awareness and connection between two people even in a small family of three can be a huge challenge.

"The roots of a lasting relationship are mindfulness, deep listening and loving speech, and a strong community to support you."

-Thich Nhat Hanh

Mindfulness is a natural human capacity to sustain open, reflective awareness of our body-mind-speech-action and environment moment by moment, with kind and wise attention. Awareness in its untainted or undefiled state can be described as the unbiased mirror like clear seeing and direct knowing faculty of the mind. Buddha described awareness (called mindfulness) as one of the five spiritual faculties or traits we need to develop for awakening. The seat or heart of awareness (*citta*), described as the radiant mind by the Buddha, is luminous, undefiled, empty, open, naturally free, and without obstruction.

Becoming self-aware of this clearly comprehending faculty of awareness (*sati sampajanna*) and establishing it in our habitually reactive mind-body consciousness (*nama rupa*) is the way to end all separation, ignorance, and suffering. The more we train our ordinary mind full of mental chatter with breath-body awareness, the more calm, non-reactive, accepting and loving the mind becomes. This unbounded non clinging love, loving-kindness or friendliness is called *metta* (Pali) or *maitri* (Sanskrit). Dipa Ma said, "Mindfulness is *metta*." This simple description resonates with my informal understanding of mindfulness.

Mindfulness develops self-awareness, non-judgement, self-regulation, and capacity to let go. The methodology of Buddhist psychology is based on remembering using awareness, introspection, and self-observation. According to the Buddha while initially unreliable, one's mind can be trained, calmed, and cultivated so as to make introspection a refined and reliable method. This methodology is the foundation for the personal insight into the nature of the mind, self, and reality the Buddha is said to have achieved.

My own view of meditation as education for the mind resonates with meditation teacher Munindraji. I recall meeting him with my father in Bodh Gaya in the early 1970s.

> *"Meditation is not only sitting; it is a way of living.*
> *It should be integrated with our whole life. It is actually*
> *an education in how to see, how to hear, how to smell,*
> *how to eat, how to drink, how to walk with full awareness.*
> *To develop mindfulness is the most important factor*
> *in the process of awakening."*
> -Living This Life Fully: Stories and
> Teachings of Munindra

Awareness remains free, unattached, non-reactive and empty like open sky. As such, when our mind becomes calm, we can directly observe, know, and see things as they are without distortion like a clear mirror without interest and involvement in mind's judgements, concepts, and evaluations.

Remembering and establishing this faculty of awareness and wise source attention (*yoniso manasikara*) into four dimensions of the mind is called the Four Foundations of Mindfulness (*samma sati*).

> *"Monks, the four kinds of mindfulness meditation are*
> *the path to (progressive) unification of mind. They are*
> *to purify sentient beings, to get past sorrow and crying,*
> *to make an end of pain and sadness, to end the cycle of*
> *suffering, and to realize extinguishment."*
> -Nibbana

1. One meditates by observing an aspect of the Body—keen, aware, and mindful, rid of desire and aversion for the world.

2. One meditates observing an aspect of Feeling—keen, aware, and mindful, rid of desire and aversion for the world.

3. One meditates observing an aspect of the Mind—keen, aware, and mindful, rid of desire and aversion for the world.

4. One meditates observing an aspect of *Dhamma* principles—keen, aware, and mindful, rid of desire and aversion for the world.

Observing the body includes mindfulness of:

1. Breathing

2. Postures (sitting, standing, walking, lying down)

3. Contextual awareness of the body in movement (eating, drinking, chewing, going forward, coming back, taking shower, cooking, cleaning, peeling eggs, talking, staying silent, and such)

4. Repulsiveness of thirty-two body parts

5. Elements as parts of the body like earth, air, water, fire elements, plus space and consciousness

6. Charnel ground corpse and death contemplation. Observe reality as it is, without grasping or pushing away.

Observing the feeling includes noticing an aspect of feeling (pleasant, painful, or neutral) as it arises and ceases in reaction to contact of six senses (sight, sound, smell, sound, touch, and mind) with sense objects. The contact may be internal, external, or both. One discerns material feeling as material feeling and spiritual feeling as spiritual. Mindfulness of feeling is established to the extent necessary for knowledge and awareness.

Observing the mind includes noticing an aspect, quality, or state of mind as it arises and ceases after some time, internally, externally, and both internally and externally. You know a mind with greed as a mind with greed, mind without greed as a mind without greed. Similarly one notices distracted mind and focused mind, hateful mind with ill will and mind of goodwill and love, expanded mind and contracted mind, dark mind and bright mind, dull mind and sharp mind, gross mind and sublime mind, depressed mind and cheerful mind, unified mind of samadhi and scattered mind, freed mind, and fettered mind, and so on.

Each mental state is liable to arise and vanish depending on external, internal, and both external and internal causes and conditions. Clinging to them as permanent or me, mine, or myself brings suffering. Practice seeing them as passing clouds in the open sky and harmless if we let them go and do not cling to thoughts, views, and beliefs.

Observing dharma (principles or qualities of mind, nature, life) includes that which hinders or supports mental development, happiness, and liberation.

The five hindrances are clinging to:

1. Sensual desire
2. Ill will

3. Sloth and torpor (low physical and mental vitality)
4. Restlessness and remorse
5. Doubt (lack of confidence in the Buddhadharma), trust in teacher (Buddha) and trust in your own abilities

You know in your practice when these states obstruct your practice. By using right understanding, antidotes, and right effort, you can overcome these hindrances to build competence in practice.

The five aggregates (constituents of personality self) are:

1. Form
2. Feeling
3. Perception
4. Conditioned habits
5. Consciousness.

Note the changing nature of each and train the mind not to cling to any of them as "I, me, or myself," which causes so much suffering and pain. Do not take anything personally, even one's own neurotic thinking and behavior, let alone the thinking and behavior of others.

Bahiya's awakening

Bahiya the householder, sailor and ascetic practitioner requested three times for a brief teaching from the Buddha with an urgency to awaken as he was approaching death. Bahiya awakened fully as an arahant just by listening to the Buddha's brief teaching on training the senses.

*"In what is seen, there is only the seen. In what is heard,
there is only the heard. In what is sensed, there is only
the sensed. In what is cognized, there is only the cognized.
This, Bahiya, is how you should train yourself. When for
you, Bahiya, there is: In the seen, only the seen. In the
heard, only the heard. In the sensed, only the sensed. In
the cognized, only the cognized. Then, Bahiya, there is
no you in connection to that. And when there is no you in
connection to that. There is no you there. And when there
is no you there, in connection to that, there is no you there.
And when there is no you there. You are neither here nor
there. Nor in-between the two. This, just this,
is the end of suffering."*
-Bahiya sutta, Udana 1.12

Upon hearing the words of the Buddha Bahiya's mind cleared. Clinging and grasping, greed and aversion ended, and all self-referential views were extinguished

The seven awakening factors

The following list is part of the list of the 37 factors of Awakening. The seven factors usually bring energy, enthusiasm and simultaneous calm in our daily practice, home and work relationships. And they are instrumental in deepening sati and samadhi, transform hindrances and breaking of the fetters.

1. Mindfulness
2. Investigation of *dharma*
3. Energy (diligent effort)
4. Joy (rapture)

5. Tranquility (calm serenity)
6. Immersion (*samadhi*)
7. Equanimity (unshakable stability of mind)

One cultivates and develops each factor to the extent necessary to end suffering and ignorance and realization of the ultimate knowledge, truth, and wisdom of final enlightenment and *nibbana* (adapted from Mahasatipatthana Sutta MN 10).

Our awareness becomes like a mirror when our mind is clear, spacious, and calm. In those moments, we can directly see and know things as they are, without distortion, judgment, or projection. Mindful-awareness or *sati* is an inherent faculty that can be developed for deepening wisdom and insight.

What this means for you is

Observe the habitual thoughts and emotions as little wisps of energy and see how they condition the state of your mind and engage large parts of your narratives that run your life. Change your focus from other people to your own self and observe your own body-mind-speech habits, both externally and internally.

Seeing the empty yet powerful nature of thoughts, you begin to detach from them or guide them as needed in a wise and wholesome direction. This practice of returning from unwholesome to wholesome again and again opens the space for calm and serenity to arise. You intentionally come back to your thoughts of non-harm and goodwill and generate metta and a wholesome state to nourish your body-mind-speech.

Gathering secondary information, facts, data, or ideas is just intellectual knowledge. Wisdom is knowledge embodied through practice, like changing neural pathways in the brain through mindfulness practice. The Awakening With Ease (AWE) process is designed to initiate conscious evolution in the human body-mind-energy system and positive changes in the human brain, DNA, and epigenetics (from within) that is needed for the brain to function beyond survival fear, shame, apathy, and other addictive patterns.

Mind that is free from the pull of sensual desire, aversion, and delusion can start seeing things as they are. Buddha taught four ways of establishing our awareness within our body-mind. They are called the four recollections, establishment, or domains of awareness (four *satipatthana*) and they are awareness of the breath-body (*kaya*), awareness of contact-feeling (*vedana*), awareness of mental states (*citta*), and awareness of mental qualities (*dhamma*).

Relationship of *Sati* and Seven Factors

Mental calm and unification (*samadhi*) due to mindfulness of breathing (*anapanasati*) is one thing that, when developed and cultivated, fulfills the four *satipatthana*. And the four *satipatthana*, when developed and cultivated, fulfill the seven factors of awakening. And the seven factors, when developed and cultivated, fulfill knowledge and freedom. (SN 54.13). This was true in my experience in 1993, although I did not receive any formal meditation instruction then. I remember listening with one-pointed attention to the evening chanting of *satipatthana* at the Sarnath main temple in my teen years, following instruction from my grandma, friend of Dipa Ma.

Samatha and *vipassana* go together

Buddha is said to have identified two paramount mental qualities that arise from wholesome meditative practice (*samma sati* and *samma samadhi*):

1. *Samatha*, calm abiding, which steadies, composes, unifies, concentrates the mind
2. *Vipassanā*, insight, which enables one to see, explore, and discern "formations" (conditioned phenomena based on form, feeling, perception, volition, and consciousness—the five aggregates)

> "There is no meditative immersion
> For one without insight
> There is no insight
> For one without meditative immersion.
> With both,
> One is close to Nirvana."
> -Dhammapada 25:372

The Buddha is said to have extolled serenity and insight as conduits for attaining a progressive state of immersion (*samadhi*) leading to the unconditioned state of *nibbana*. Both serenity and insight, *samatha*, and *vipassana* went hand in hand in my experience. Five aggregates and their impermanent, unsatisfactory, and not-self nature was also observed from beginning with the inquiry, *Who am I not?* Noticing three kinds of feeling dependent on contact (vedana) with six senses—pleasant, painful, and neutral—helps to let go of grasping and clinging to feelings that cause craving and suffering.

> "The underlying obsession or tendency (anusaya) to lust/greed should be given up when it comes to pleasant feeling. The underlying tendency to repulsion/hate should be given up when it comes to painful feeling. The underlying tendency to delusion/ignorance should be given up when it comes to neutral feeling."
> -Nun Dhammadinna, culavedalla sutta, MN 44

> "When you let go, the mind becomes peaceful. When you let go even more, you become even more peaceful. What we call "jhānas" are merely signposts along that road of letting go. Someone who, when grounded in right view, practices that deep level of letting go, regardless of their status as lay or ordained, completes the factors of the path and will experience the fruit."
> -Bhante Sujato, Suttacentral.

After his awakening, the Buddha said that he had discovered a long but lost path leading to an ancient city (SN 12,65). The ancient city was Nibbana (enlightenment), the field of Noble Ones and the long-lost path was The Noble Tenfold Path, culminating in right (wholesome) knowledge and right (complete) liberation from suffering of samsara.

> "Simply put, jhana states (meditative immersion) are stages of letting go. One cannot be attached to letting go."
> -Ajahn Brahm

Breathing is the most popular focus of samatha meditation, however Buddha listed 10 other Kasinas (objects of focus) for concentration meditation: earth, water, fire, wind, blue, yellow, red, white, space and consciousness.

The Middle Way to End Ignorance

"Dhamma is beneficial in the beginning, beneficial in the middle, and beneficial in the end."
-The Buddha

- **Right Practice:** Mendicants, these two extremes should not be cultivated by one who has gone forth. Indulgence in sensual pleasures, which is low, crude, ordinary, ignoble, and unwholesome. And indulgence in self-mortification, which is painful, ignoble, and pointless. Avoiding these two extremes, the Realized One woke up by understanding the middle way of practice (the Noble 10 fold Path, including outcome), which gives vision and knowledge, and leads to peace, direct knowledge, awakening, and Nibbana. - Dhammacakkappavattana Sutta, SN 56.11

- On Right View: "The view that all exists (*sarvastivada*) is a wrong view and the view that nothing exists (emptiness) is another wrong (polarized) view. My *dhamma* avoids extreme views. I teach from the middle; I teach The Noble *Tenfold* Path as the middle way that avoids extreme views." -Kaccayanagotta Sutta

- "The middle way shows that suffering originates in dependence on ignorance. From ignorance of the

Four Noble Truths (*ariya sacca*), dependent origination and The Noble Tenfold Path as a requisite condition all sufferings arise.

- In the Upakkilesa Sutta (M128), Buddha gives the metaphor on proper holding of mind in Right Mindfulness. "Grasp a quail too tightly, and it will die then and there; but grasp the quail too loosely, and it will fly out of your hands."

- In another metaphor on Right Effort in practicing mindfulness, Buddha instructed to monk Sona (AN 6.55) on how to tune the strings of the lute for optimal sound. It is best not to be "too tight or too loose." To bring the factor of courageous effort (*viriya*) into perfect harmony with the moment, it is best not to be too striving nor too relaxed.

- The Eight Worldly Dangers are praise and blame, win and loss, pleasure and pain, and fame and shame. Each of these eight worldly conditions is subject to change, hence stressful and painful to an uninstructed ordinary person. A wise person who is well trained in *dhamma* is not afflicted by changes in these worldly conditions. She can keep her calm and equanimity in all situations until the wind of danger passes away.

- Middle way is the way of wise discernment of what is beneficial, wholesome, and skillful (*kusala*) and what is unwholesome and unskillful (*akusala*) in a given situation.

There are many other ways the middle way can be comprehended. It requires a high level of mental development and cultivation.

What this means to you is

Before embarking on a long journey into The Noble Tenfold Path, set your next step and direction in your inner GPS of awareness (intuitive heart), check your front and rear-view mirror, make a note of mental state, outside weather, amount of fuel in the tank, your starting time, your next few stops, and your intention for this sitting or walking meditation now, this week, or in the next few weeks. You are ready to adapt, adjust, and course correct for unforeseen distractions and obstacles on the way, while never losing sight of your original intention. Skillfully navigating life with our mind-body is similar to learning to drive a car, in some ways.

Mindful meditation can be understood with the analogy of driving in a crowded city for the first time. Too many distractions or hindrances in the mind may seem daunting and confusing in the beginning. Clarity of view and intention, inquiry, and energy all affect the quantity and quality of one's practice time. The more relaxed and clear you are about your view and intention for cultivating mindful awareness, the more direct the path will be, provided you are not attached to any specific outcome coming from the ego mind.

Three Marks of Existence

All created and fabricated things, all conditioned habits (*sankhara*) are impermanent (*anicca*), suffering (*dukkha*), and not-self (*anatta*)

Seeing this with insight, one becomes disenchanted with suffering
This is the path to clarity, wisdom, knowledge, and vision
The best of paths is The Noble Tenfold Path
The best of truths, the Four Noble Truths
The best of qualities is dispassion
And the best among gods and humans
Is the one with (*dhamma*) eyes to see.

-Dhammapada Ch 20 (adapted by author)

Repeated reflections on the three marks or signs of life (existence) help us detach from difficult situations and cravings. They are impermanence (*anicca*), unsatisfactoriness (*dukkha*), and the non-self (*anatta*) nature of all conditioned and created things. You can release mental stories and physical attachments (called fabrications) by practicing simple breath and body awareness meditation, *metta* meditation, or any other kind of meditation mentioned here.

The Buddha said that anything that leads to affliction (five aggregates), anything that is impermanent (five aggregates), like form, feeling, perception, mental volition. and consciousness cannot be called self. They should be seen as stressful, impermanent, and not-self (Anatta-lakkhana Sutta SN 22.59).

Buddha talks about four ways our mind perceives reality through distortions. The four Vipallasa or distortions are:

- seeing what is impermanent (changing) as permanent (unchanging),
- seeing what is painful (unsatisfying) as pleasant (satisfying),
- seeing what is without self (not-self) as self (identity), and
- seeing what is not beautiful (unattractive) as beautiful (attractive)

These distortions (inversions) are fundamental to the Buddhist understanding of ignorance or delusion leading to mental sickness. They distort at the level of senses or sensory perception, thinking habit and unwholesome view of reality. We might become so convinced that there is a snake by the path that no amount of evidence to the contrary will cause us to change our view. Only true Dhamma helps us see thing as they are and develop right vision and knowledge.

Kamma: old, new, and its ending

Kamma (*karma* in Sanskrit) simply means past, present, and future action of body, speech, and mind. *Kamma* in Buddhism originates with mental intentions (even if no physical action is carried out) and volitions arising from old, conditioned habits (*sankhara* created by ignorance). Negative thoughts, ill will, anger, etc. has negative fruits and positive wholesome intentions and volition bring positive results. So thoughts of killing, harming, pride, jealousy, and anger all bear negative fruit if continued for a long time.

There are four kinds of *kamma*. There is dark *kamma* with dark ripening, there is bright *kamma* with bright ripening, there is dark-and-bright *kamma* with dark-and-bright ripening, and there is *kamma* that is not dark and not bright with neither dark-nor-bright ripening that leads to the end or fading away of *kamma*. *Kamma* is carried forward from moment to moment by mindstream (made of gross, fine, and subtle consciousness and energy), even after the death of the physical body.

> *"Students, beings are owners of kammas, heirs of kammas, they have kammas as their progenitor, kammas as their kin, kammas as their homing-place. It is kammas that differentiate beings according to inferiority and superiority."*
> *-Kamma sutta (SN 35.146)*

Kamma is not deterministic as people can make a different choice and intention at any moment. Most people have mixed *kammas*. There are stories in Buddha's lifetime of many people waking up despite bad situations. There was the story of a notorious bandit and serial killer Angulimala, who killed 999 people but failed to kill the Buddha. His mind shifted after being unable to come close to the Buddha. After seeing the Buddha's fearless light and hearing his kind words, he instantly came to his senses, became a disciple, and soon become enlightened.

People often have partial views and misunderstandings about *kamma*, because *kamma* is not the only thing that impacts our lives. It is due to not knowing kamma that beings keep wandering in *samsara*, and worse, fall below the human plane to planes of pain and deprivation.

The Buddha said, "And what, monks, is the way leading to the cessation of *kamma*? It is this Noble Tenfold Path; that is, right (wholesome) view, right intention, right speech, right action, right livelihood, right effort, right mindfulness, right concentration, right knowledge, and right liberation."

What this means for you: Think before you speak or act. Watch the effect of wrong and right action in your own life and relationship with your friends or siblings. Intentions make a difference in how you respond to any situation. Same actions taken with a mind of goodwill and kindness have a different impact than actions taken with anger and delusion. The Buddha told his seven-year-old son, Rāhula, "If you feel no shame at telling a deliberate lie, you're totally empty of goodness." Reflect often on your actions or inactions and if they are harmful to others and you. Appropriate and mindful action requires wise attention and intention.

Overflowing with merit (*punna*)

Punna is an important idea in Buddhist praxis and ethics. It is a beneficial and protective energy which accumulates in one's karmic bank due to good deeds, thoughts, words, and intentions. Merit can be gained through purity of mind and also practice of generosity, virtue, meditation, and wisdom. *Punna* attracts good fortune, prosperity, and protection from gods and humans in this life and aids in good rebirth and growth toward enlightenment. The opposite of *punna* is *papa* (demerit) for breaking five ethical codes of conducts (abstaining from killing, stealing, sexual misconduct, lying, and taking drugs and intoxicants that make one heedless).

CHAPTER 8

Awaken

"Human beings come to this world to do particular work.
That work is the purpose, and each is specific to the person.
If you remember everything else and forget this, then you will
have done nothing in your life."

-Rumi

"Science cannot solve the ultimate mystery of nature. And that
is because, in the last analysis, we ourselves are a part of the
mystery that we are trying to solve. All matter originates and
exists only by virtue of a force. We must assume behind this
force the existence of a conscious and intelligent Mind.
This Mind is the matrix of all matter."

-Max Planck

The Buddha asked his chief disciple, Sariputta, "Now what is ignorance, what is the origin of ignorance, what is the cessation of ignorance and what is the way of practice out of ignorance?"

Sariputta said, "Not having knowledge of stress (dukkha), not having knowledge of the origin of stress, not having knowledge of ending stress, and not having knowledge of the way of practice leading to end of stress. This is called ignorance. The path to end ignorance is The Noble Tenfold

Path. American historian Daniel J. Boorstin said, "The greatest obstacle to discovery is not ignorance, but the illusion of knowledge."

At the end of the path, the superpower mindful awareness is practiced through still immersion practice called *samma samadhi*. It is possible to reach the end by deep understanding of the first two wholesome path factors, right view, and right intention. Each path factor builds on and is conditioned by the previous ones. In my view, the order of path factors are important because they follow the natural order or sequence in the development, evolution, and involution of mind and consciousness. All things are energy and vibration. Every physical (and mental) phenomena we experience has an unseen, non-physical, formless, energetic, vibrational aspect in consciousness and energy as stated by Einstein in his famous equation: $E=mc^2$. Mass came out of energy and light.

Awakening from the illusion to reality

In *buddhadharma*, the original sin can be seen as the original ignorance of consciousness getting identified and entangled with name and forms (the five skandhas). By withdrawing our five senses from the world of forms and turning inward, we begin to reclaim the wise source attention (*yoniso manasikara*) and non-reactive natural awareness not identified with names and forms. Historical Buddha affirmed the preciousness of human birth in spite of a finite lifespan afflicted by pain of birth, sickness, old age, death, contact with the unpleasant, and getting the unwanted. Since we have both pleasure and pain in this human realm, unlike the divine realms of refined pleasures, we have a better opportunity to awaken through our suffering and our own right effort.

In my own direct experience, when I was going through lot of pain and uncertainty after resigning from my planning job, I remembered the sense of unbounded joy and adventure I felt when I got the gift of *The Children's Book of Knowledge*. I was completely filled with wonder and awe while reading about great events in history and biographies of people. I instantly recognized my wholesome passion for learning, discovery, and knowledge.

Chanda (as opposed to *tanha*) is the wholesome desire that arises from wisdom and wise attention. Since my goal was knowledge and vision for this life and ending suffering by ending doubt, self-view, and ignorance, my mind was wide open, curious, and pliable. It became progressively still, empty, and immersed in a unified flow state and singularly focused on knowing the unconditioned. In my self-guided practice and quest for knowledge (gnosis), I was pragmatic to include both my knowledge of science and direct experience as an observer.

As a panelist in "Teaching Dhamma in New Lands" 'in the 2012 Conference of International Association of Buddhist Universities (IABU) in Thailand, I put together my thoughts in a paper titled, "Bridging Science and Spirituality Through Buddha's Middle Way to Knowledge." I had the instant recognition before embarking on The Noble Eightfold Path that if knowledge is divided and not integrated in our heart-minds and brains, the world will be split, fragmented, and lost in the nightmare dream of separation, confusion, and conflicts. Through meditative immersion, we have the capacity to merge with our fifth dimensional universal mind and consciousness. In advanced stages of meditation (*jhanas*), we can merge our awareness of the unbounded infinite space, progressively filled with *metta*, mass and energy, energy and consciousness, and consciousness and light.

In my mind, I made the connection that ancient Indian science was based on the science of consciousness (*vijnana*), because both science and consciousness have the exact same word, "*vijnana*," to this day. In Buddhist thought, *vijnana* is the six sense bases. Mind is the sixth sense or inner eye (*dhamma chakku*). We need to open and develop insight into the nature of reality. Greed, hate, and delusion are temporary defilements coming from wounded and unhealed ego lost in the dream of scarcity, limitation, competition, and separation from the source or unified quantum zero field.

According to the Heart Math Institute, The heart is the most powerful source of electromagnetic energy in the human body, producing the largest rhythmic electromagnetic field of any of the body's organs. The heart's electrical field is about sixty times greater in amplitude and one hundred times stronger than the electrical activity and field generated by the brain. Interestingly, in Buddhism, the heart-mind (*citta*) is seen as the primary seat of mind. Heart-mind cannot be separated from the living electromagnetic field of the cosmos, except by our false identification with body-mind (separate ego self).

Right worldview and Intention

We urgently need a worldview coming from direct experiential knowledge and truth of reality (non-conceptual) through:

1. Mindfulness of affliction (*dukkha/klesha*) in body-mind-speech-nervous system, and in social-institutional-work place traumas with kindness and wisdom
2. Origin of all suffering (*samudaya*) through ignorance of dependent origination links (*paticcasamuppada*)
3. Ending of all suffering (*nirodha*) through knowledge of transcendental or reverse dependent origination
4. Path (*magga*) to end suffering (*dukkha*) by ending ignorance (*avijja*); The Noble Tenfold Path, ending with supreme wisdom, knowledge, and complete liberation (*nibbana*)

This worldview supports mindful ethical living, respect for all life and earth relations, an attitude of friendliness, inner peace, and openness to other cultures and value systems. Would there be mass shooting and police brutality on people of color or unnecessary violent war between nation states, where citizens voluntarily take the five ethical restraints of body-mind-speech to create psychological safety and trust in their homes, workplace, and communities. The Noble Tenfold Path is the middle way to ultimate knowledge and freedom that bridges the gap between science and spirituality and paves the way to self-liberating spiritual science of super-consciousness.

Using the inner technology of awareness, we can reimagine to balance our highly imbalanced man-made systems and nurture our mind-body potential by organizing intentional communities to fulfill our highest aspiration for peace, happiness, truth, and freedom. Buddha went to the very source of human suffering and ignorance and found a way out through developing the five spiritual faculties (the power of faith, energy, awareness, concentration, and wisdom) which culminated in the freedom of *nirvana*, emptiness (*sunyata*), and signlessness.

On an individual level, right view starts with establishing your worldview of life and existence from your own human journey and quest for freedom, wisdom, and truth. To learn, we need to be like an empty cup, unlearning some disempowering myths and core beliefs from time to time that keeps us stuck in the wheel of suffering. Also, keep the mind open to learn more than you know from other wise and enlightened beings. Our heart-mind is naturally inclined toward knowledge and right understanding.

> *"The greatest obstacle to discovery is not ignorance—it is the illusion of knowledge."*
> -Daniel J. Boorstein

What this means to you

Connect the dots and bridge the gaps in your own understanding and view of the world. Never lose sight of your own experiential journey into non-conceptual wisdom. Wisdom is embodied knowledge. We activate inherent wisdom and natural intelligence by connecting with breath, body-mind sensation, and establishing awareness in the four domains of body, feeling, mind, and principles of *dhamma*. This will help you to sustain a calm, clear, alert, and healthy mental state.

Everything in life changes, nothing remains the same. This is called the truth of impermanence (*anicca*). All changing things are unsatisfactory (*dukkha*), and as such, there is no permanent self or unchanging soul (*anatta*). What we conventionally call "self" is actually a flowing stream of consciousness made of five aggregates (*nama-rupa*) made of form (*rupa*), feeling (*vedana*), perception (*sanna*), mental disposition (*sankhara*), and consciousness (*vijnana*). *Sankhara* (mental formation and fabrications) is related to our karmic habits and cultural traits (like the culture of aggression, violence, and supremacy). *Sankharas* are conditionings and all conditioned things are impermanent (*anicca*).

The *trilakkhana* (three characteristic marks) of existence appear in Pali texts as, "*sabbe sankhara anicca, sabbe sankhara dukkha, sabbe dhamma anatta.*" It is by complete understanding and seeing of *anicca*, *dukkha*, and *anatta* (not-self) with wisdom that one is able to rid oneself of the accumulated *samkhara* (volitional habits) and dukkha in one's own karmic mindstream. The Buddha's advice to monks is that they maintain the awareness of *anicca*, *dukkha*, and *anatta* in all four body positions (sitting, walking, standing, and lying). Repeating anything before falling asleep takes it to our subconscious and makes it easier to remember and recall.

Metta as the base of mindfulness

The underlying force of craving and aversion in our mind can be tamed by cultivating the basic practice of goodwill and friendliness toward our own difficulties and all living beings. Just like the warm glow of morning sun, imagine a radiating lamp in your heart, infusing your whole body and mind. Put a little inner smile in your heart and also in your face, like your favorite Buddha image. It is quite difficult to progress in practice with aversion or fixed expectation of any kind. A sense of wonder and adventure is helpful.

"Mindfulness is love (metta). Enlightenment is great love."
-Dipama

Stay focused on one practice for two to three weeks until you feel a definite subtle shift in your consciousness and energy. Usually a sense of lightness, calm, and bubbling happiness you may have lost in the past few months or years returns. Metta helps us develop spaciousness, greater acceptance of the present moment, sustain a wholesome state, and initiate more compassionate inquiry into the things we tend to avoid or resist investigating. *Metta* done correctly will turn naturally into unbounded compassion, compassion into unbounded sympathetic joy, and joy into unbounded equanimity.

"Even as a mother protects with her life her child, her only child, so with a boundless heart should one cherish all living beings, radiating kindness over the entire world. Spreading upward to the skies, and downward to the depths; outward and unbounded, freed from hatred and ill-will."
-The Buddha, in Metta Keraniya Sutta

The Metta Keraniya Sutta (AN 11.16) describes the benefit of *metta* meditation as:

1. You sleep easily
2. You have pleasant dreams
3. People love you
4. *Devas* (gods, angels), animals love you
5. *Devas* will protect you
6. External dangers, such as poisons, weapons, and fire, will not harm you
7. Your face will be radiant
8. Your mind will be serene
9. You will die unconfused
10. You will be born in happy realms

Bodhicitta resolve

"The power of one is above all things the power to believe in yourself, often well beyond any latent ability you may have previously demonstrated."
-Bryce Courtenay

"Just as the great ocean has one taste, the taste of salt, so also this teaching and discipline has one taste, the taste of liberation."
-The Buddha, in the Udana

Bodhi means awakening and *citta* means heart. The deep aspiration to awaken, awaken for the benefit of all beings spontaneously arises with the practice of the unbounded and immeasurable states of mind called *brahmaviharas*.

These four sublime and infinite states are *metta* (love), *karuna* (compassion), *mudita* (sympathetic joy), and *upekkha* (equanimity). Behind this altruistic aspiration lies the intention to serve and save all beings from suffering with wisdom and compassion. The upward wish for realization of the ultimate wisdom in the absolute join with the compassion to serve all beings in the relative.

Equanimity is the goal of mental development with meditation. It is the fourth sublime divine state (*brahmaviharas*). When equanimity is very deep, continuous, and stable, the mind can reach unified stillness of wholesome *samadhi* (*samatha-vipassana-jhana*) of infinite space, infinite consciousness, infinite nothingness, and finally, the unshakable or imperturbable state of neither perception nor non-perception (highest state in formless meditation). By non-grasping and non-identification even this exalted state of mind one can break through to the unconditioned, full awakening of *nibbana*.

The Chinese image of female *bodhisattva* (*Guan Yin*) of compassion with royal ease with her one leg in seated position and another ready to move forward depicts this graceful power to move between the two worlds. With this resolve, if sincerity and equanimity is established, you could be connected to the field of noble ones in the unseen.

Bodhicitta arises when one meditates spreading a heart full of love (*metta*) to one direction, and to the second, and to the third, and to the fourth. In the same way above, below, across, everywhere, all around, s(he) spreads a heart full of compassion (*karuna*) to the suffering in the whole world—abundant, expansive, limitless, free of enmity and ill will. Compassion turns to unbounded empathic joy (*mudita*).

Going beyond fear, doubt, and identity-view

Meditation is really a process of relaxing all the resistance we have accumulated in our body-mind and letting go of any wanting. Be in a state of receptivity. As long as the wanting and craving mind is involved, the self is in the way. Mind goes to deeper levels of *samadhi* and *jhana* by itself and it reveals its deeper dimension if we are not trying to control or force it anyway.

Personally speaking I had no instruction in meditation or mindfulness when I started on the path. With a few basic teachings, a compassionate inquiry process, and inner knowledge, I could sustain my practice for seven months by staying with the four movements of the whole body, while taking care of a child and spouse as a full-time mom, wife, and big sister in the Bengali student community. Within the first two to three weeks of focusing on relaxed breathing, I started to feel a sense of ease and relaxation in my body I had not felt in a long time. With a more calm and coherent heart-mind, I became interested in exploring more.

> "the knowing self is not born; it does not die. it has not
> sprung from anything; nothing has sprung from it.
> birthless, eternal, everlasting and ancient,
> it is not killed when the body is killed."
> -Katha Upanishad

The seven factors of awakening, four domains of mindful-awareness, *samatha-vipassana*, five *skandhas*, The Noble Tenfold Path, a simpler version of dependent origination, and the unshakable intention to reach the unconditioned, all appeared naturally one by one in my practice. I was in a state of flow and had no hindrance (I did not learn about it until many years later). In positive psychology, a flow state, also known colloquially as "being in the zone," is the mental state in which a person performing some activity is fully immersed in a feeling of energized focus, full involvement, and enjoyment in the process of the activity. Immersion or samadhi gives rise to a flow state of bliss. In my humble view, the goal for all Buddhist practitioners, no matter what path or tradition, needs to be stream entry (*sotapanna*).

The Four Stages of Awakening and the Ten Fetters

The map of the four stages of awakening is central to the early Buddhist schools, including Theravada. The Four stages of Awakening, in early Buddhism and Theravada, are four progressive stages that lead to freedom from various fetters (chains), culminating in full awakening (*bodhi*) as an arahant within the support structure of the four-fold *sangha*. Pacceka Buddhas are solitary and awaken individually when there is no Buddha or *sangha*.

These four stages are *sotapanna* (stream-enterer), *sakadagami* (once-returner), *anagami* (non-returner), and *arahant* (deathless). The oldest Buddhist texts portray the Buddha as referring to people who are at one of these four stages as noble people (*ariya-puggala*) and the community of such awakened persons as the noble sangha (ariya-sangha). The world is ripe now with new cosmic energies coming to the planet for the first time for spontaneous awakenings and the arising of a noble sangha.

Ten Fetters

The Buddha described the awakening or liberation from suffering and ignorance in terms of ten mental fetters, chains, or bonds (samyojana) that shackles a sentient being to the illusion of samsara, the cycle of repeated lives with stress, craving, and pain. By cutting through all the fetters, on the spiritual path, one attains to full awakening to the deathless (nibbana).

The Pali canon's Sutta Pitaka identifies "ten fetters of becoming:"

1. Belief in a self (sakkāya-diṭṭhi)
2. Doubt or uncertainty (vicikiccha), about the Buddha and his dhamma
3. Attachment to rites and rituals (sīlabbata-parāmāsa)

The stream enterer (sotapanna) breaks the first three chains and attains the dhamma-eye, an intuitive grasp of the dhamma, glimpse of nibbana, unshakable confidence in buddhadharma, and never falls to lower than human realm. Attain final awakening in this or seven lifetimes at the most.

1. Craving for sensual desire (kamachando)
2. Ill will (vyapado)

The once-returner to the human realm (*sakadagami*) weakens craving and ill will substantially, and the non-returner (*anagami*) uproots both completely. The latter is born in pureland heavens and attains *nibbana* there.

1. Craving for material existence, rebirth in a form realm (*ruparago*)
2. Craving for immaterial existence, rebirth in a formless realm (*aruparago*)
3. Conceit (*mana*)
4. Restlessness (*uddhacca*)
5. Ignorance (*avijja*)

Arahat uproots the higher five fetters and completes the holy life and never returns to human or any other planes. All four stages end with supramundane attainments and are irreversible. According to Dhammawiki, there are about 3,000 lay sotapannas mentioned in the Pali Canon, at least 90 sakadagamis, at least 500 anagamis, and a few lay arahants mentioned in the Theravada Commentaries and at least one case in the Pali Canon (Vinaya).

Thirty-one planes of existence

In Buddhist cosmology, there are thirty-one planes of rebirth and evolution in samsara for beings to transmigrate to upward or downward according to their *karma*, intention, and worldview. The realms of existence are customarily divided into three distinct worlds (*loka*), listed here in descending order of refinement and density:

- The Formless Immaterial World (*arupa-loka*) consists of four realms that are accessible to those who pass away while meditating in the infinite formless *jhanas* (infinite, space, infinite consciousness, infinite nothingness and infinite neither perception nor non-perception)

- The Fine-Material Form World (*rupa-loka*) consists of sixteen realms whose inhabitants (*devas*) experience extremely refined degrees of mental pleasure. These realms are accessible to those who have attained at least some level of *jhana* (meditative immersion) and who have thereby managed to (temporarily) suppress hatred and ill-will.

- They are said to possess extremely refined bodies of pure light. The highest of these realms, the pure abodes, are accessible only to those who have attained to non-returning, the third stage of awakening. The Fine-Material World and the Immaterial World together constitute the heavens (*sagga*) consisting of twenty planes of *brahmas* (supreme deities) and six planes of *devas*, above humans.

- The Sensuous World (*kama-loka*) consists of eleven realms in which experience—both pleasurable and not—is dominated by the five senses. Seven of these realms are favorable destinations and include our own human realm (fifth plane) as well as several realms occupied by *devas*. The lowest realms are the four "bad" destinations, which include the titan and demons (*asura*), hungry ghost (*preta*), animal, and hell realms.

The goal of awakening is to stop falling to lower than human planes and lead a noble *Arya* life of generosity, virtue, and meditative wisdom for the benefit of all beings. As Nikola Tesla said, "If you want to find the secrets of the universe, think in terms of energy, frequency, and vibration."

Power of enlightened consciousness

Using forty years of research in kinesiology (muscle testing), Dr. David R. Hawkins, in his book *Power Vs. Force*, calibrates human consciousness levels for different mental-emotional-behavioral states. Only 5% of people on the planet function at the level of 500 (unconditional love) and above and 85% function below the level of courage, 200. One individual at level 300 counterbalances 90,000 individuals below level 200.

- 1 person at level 500 (love) counterbalances 750,000 people < 200 level
- 1 person at level 600 (peace) counterbalances 10 million people < 200 level
- 1 person at level 700 (enlightenment) counterbalances 70 million people <200
- 12 persons at 700 equal one avatar (Jesus, Krishna, or Buddha) at level 1,000

Many scientists calibrate at level 400 and above but cannot make it to unconditional love of *metta*. Einstein calibrated at 499. It means your effort and practice toward transforming low consciousness energy attractors has a powerful beneficial impact both on personal and planetary level. You can see the enormous power of peace at 600 over the power of fear operating below the level of courage at 200.

What this means for you

If you forget everything in this book, just remember to: *Be love and live love. Do it without clinging, aversion, and identification.* Love is simply a harmonious field of resonance. Love and treat yourself regularly with kindness, especially through difficult lonely times and reach out to good people or even a stranger if you need help or simple connection. Loving-kindness is the great force of healing, reconciliation, co-creation, regeneration, release from old negative *kamma*, and restoration of hope for humanity in this world. Altruistic love allows us to grow beyond comfort zones, overcome fear, be brave, generous, and use our resources and creativity to go beyond any limitation and serve any and all beings. It is also the great antidote for ill will, hate, war, cruelty, apathy, violence, cynicism, domination, control, manipulation, and judgements.

From ignorance to knowledge of liberation

The Upanisa Sutta (SN 12:23) gives many iterations of the twelve links of causation and conditionality from ignorance to suffering and suffering to knowledge of liberation of heart (*ceto vimutti*). The second part is called transcendental dependent arising (*lokuttara paticcasamuppada*).

"Thus, monks, ignorance is the vital supporting condition for *kamma* formations (*sankhara*), *kamma* formations are the supporting condition for consciousness, consciousness is the supporting condition for mentality-materiality, mentality-materiality is the supporting condition for the sixfold sense base, the sixfold sense base is the supporting condition for contact, contact is the supporting condition for feeling, feeling is the supporting condition for craving, craving is the supporting condition for clinging, clinging is the supporting condition for existence, existence is the supporting condition for birth, and birth is the supporting condition for suffering (of aging, sickness, death, getting what one does not want and so forth)."

It is important to mention that ignorance in modern age shows up socially and at workplaces as deep-seated, often unconscious biases, prejudices, and oppression (external and internal) fueled by fears, entitlements, myths, and privileges of one group over another. The Buddha is also considered an evolutionary social reformer who challenged the Brahmin orthodoxy, their privileged status and authority of *vedas* in the four-tiered caste system, which denied individual autonomy and human freedom.

He also proclaimed the equal capacity of women to be enlightened to the highest level. He created the oldest nuns order (*bhikkhuni sangha*), following the third request from his aunt and foster mother, Mahapajapati, five years after establishing the monks order. The paradox of power, privilege, wealth, and status is that they can keep us comfortable and ignorant about the social realities of oppression, racism, colonization, marginalization of BIPOC, women, immigrants, underprivileged, and the poor.

Recognition of suffering is the supporting condition for faith (*saddha*), conviction, and commitment to Buddha and his enlightened teachings. Faith is the supporting condition for joy, joy is the supporting condition for rapture, rapture is the supporting condition for tranquility, tranquility is the supporting condition for happiness, happiness is the supporting condition for concentration, concentration is the supporting condition for the knowledge and vision of things as they really are, the knowledge and vision of things as they really are is the supporting condition for disenchantment, disenchantment is the supporting condition for dispassion, dispassion is the supporting condition for emancipation, and emancipation is the supporting condition for the knowledge of the destruction (of the defilements or cankers of greed, hate, and delusion)."

Buddha advised Dighavu, a lay disciple, who was sick, suffering and gravely ill, but already grounded in faith of the triple gem, and four factors of stream-entry (association with the wise, listening to the true Dhamma, wise attention and practicing true dhamma) as such: "You should further develop these six things that play a part in realization. You should dwell contemplating the impermanence of all (physical and mental) formations, perceiving suffering in what is impermanent, perceiving non-self in what is suffering, perceiving abandonment, perceiving dispassion, perceiving cessation."

Part III

"Ananda, be islands unto yourselves, refuges unto yourselves, seeking no external refuge; with the Dhamma as
your island, the Dhamma as your refuge, seeking no other
refuge. ...When One dwells contemplating the body in the
body, earnestly, clearly comprehending, and mindfully,
after having overcome desire and sorrow in regard to the
world; when he dwells contemplating feelings in feelings,
the mind in the mind, and dharmas in Dharma,... truly, he
is an island unto himself, a refuge unto himself, seeking
no external refuge; having the Dhamma as his island, the
Dhamma as his refuge, seeking no other refuge."

-The Buddha's last words in Mahaparinibbana Sutta
(DN 16)

CHAPTER 9

Conclusion

❧

"This is peace, this is exquisite—the resolution of all fabrications, the relinquishment of all acquisitions, the ending of craving, dispassion, cessation, and nibbana."

-AN 3.32

The awareness and knowledge of the possibility of Awakening With Ease (AWE) is every human's birthright. I promised you would know the immeasurable benefit of turning your wise attention and awareness inward. I delivered within the limitations of language and words. You just learned the simplified six foundations of AWE for modern seekers and contemplatives and connected skillfully with the vast teachings of the Buddha and my own direct experience.

No matter where you are in your journey, I can help you go further. Awakening is a primordial evolutionary impulse that exists deep within every human heart-mind and can be accessed by using loving awareness of the heart's intuitive intelligence, mind's wholesome inner knowing, and the inherent wisdom and intelligence of the life-force (*chi, prana, qi, spirit, aura, vital energy*) flowing through us. We just have to learn to be in sync with it through mindful meditation.

It is from not having the mindful vision of the Four Noble Truths (direct recognition and realization) of life as subject to many stress, the causes of stress, the ending of stress, and The Noble Tenfold Path, leading to the ultimate realization of the supramundane knowledge of total liberation from stress (*nibbana*) that we as mortals kept wandering and transmigrating in samsara for millennia fettered by ignorance, doubt, self-view, and hindered by craving, confusion, and suffering. By the intent and merit of reading and comprehension of this book, and the practice of the six "A" steps, may you in the least attain the fruit of stream-entry (*sotapanna*) never again destined for the lower realms (hell, animal wombs, hungry ghosts, planes of misfortune and deprivation), headed for self-awakening.

With the right vision of *dharma*, confidence in Buddha and yourself, and wholesome intention to end ignorance, you are set in the right direction. Do not believe in any of your own or others' disempowering thoughts, beliefs, perception, and habits. Give up any extreme, reductionist or dualistic view. Practice the wholesome middle way of skillful discernment, loving-awareness, ethical action, peace, and equanimity. Concentrate on your wholesome wish for total liberation and ultimate truth for the benefit of all beings. That's all there is to it.

"Oneself indeed is one's own protector
What other protector could there be?
With self-control
One gains a protector hard to obtain.

Harm is done by oneself alone;
By oneself is one defiled;
Evil is avoided by oneself

By oneself alone is one purified.
Purity and pollution depend on oneself;
No one can purify another."
-Dhammapada 12: 160-165

Awakening and enlightenment is a path of conscious choice and conscious evolution. We choose to leave the fixed and separate identity-view, survival fear of ego, and its harmful conceptual constructs based on external greed for power (over others), sex, wealth, cravings, and wrong views. AWE is a transformational education for the highest development of human mind and psyche. This self-training prepares your mind to develop the skillful virtues of mindfulness, wisdom, compassion, awake self-leadership, confidence, creativity, and resilience.

Conventional education

Our formal schooling focuses only on the intellect, achievement of the self or personality (*sakkayaditthi*), and secondary information and does not teach anything about the human heart. We neglect the powerful, experiential side of the human journey and purpose, and most importantly, how to relate, understand, use, and direct the energy of our feelings, thoughts, and emotions in a wholesome positive direction. Learn to discern the mental-emotional states, where not only craving and aversion arise, but also unbounded love, compassion, joy, and equanimity arise. With regular practice, you are able to guide and choose your state of mind, thought, feeling tones, health, and wellness.

The Buddha addressed many delusions, wrong views, and biases of his time as they distort the fundamental truths about our world. We as responsible and engaged citizens and Dhamma practitioners need to do the same through mindful dialogue in inclusive sangha spaces led by diverse leaders. We can all embrace the higher consciousness of unbounded love (*metta*), forgiveness, wisdom, and compassion (*karuna*) to restore, repair, regenerate, and replenish all our interdependent relationships with all beings and the natural world. Buddha used his own powers of observation and mental faculties, both intellect and intuitive insight, to guide him to his own enlightenment for the benefit of humankind and all beings. He advised us to do the same.

"Of all types of corruption, ignorance is the worst. Having abandoned this corruption, monks, and good practitioners of dhamma remain corruption free"
-The Buddha.

This book is about ending suffering by ending spiritual ignorance (*avijja*) or unawareness. It also gives a clear view of awakening, what processes are needed to awaken from ignorance to the knowledge and vision of both the individual and collective liberation and happiness by the supreme meditative (*samadhi*), realization of *sunnyata* or voidness of self, and the world of five aggregates and six sense spheres. A new paradigm based on love and right understanding replaces and uproots the egoic paradigm of greed, hate, war, and delusion. If everyone reading this book makes an intention to live and embody some of the teachings and the six "A" steps (alive, ask, abandon, accept, aware, and awake) shared here, we can collectively realize that we are already living in a heaven called Earth.

More on *nibbana* (unbinding)

Nibbana names the transcendent and singularly ineffable freedom that stands as the final and highest potential of humanity and the ultimate goal of all of the Buddha's teachings.

> There's no fire like lust,
> No misfortune like hate,
> No pain like the aggregates,
> No happiness higher than peace.
> Hunger is the foremost illness.
> Sankharas the foremost suffering
> For one knowing this truth
> As it actually is,
> Nirvana is the foremost happiness.
> Health is the foremost possession,
> Contentment, the foremost wealth.
> Trust; the foremost kinship,
> Unbinding, the foremost ease.
>
> -Dhammapada, Ch 15, 202-204

What this means for you

Do you feel inspired to be part of a peaceful (r)evolution in consciousness, part of the noble guardians and mindful awake leaders protecting the people, planet, and all beings with courage, wisdom, and compassion? Can you imagine a *maha sangha* of kind peaceful warriors in the seen and unseen, working quietly for the sake of realizing the ultimate inner freedom from fear, ignorance, and suffering? Small intentional communities living in harmony and practicing mindful meditation and true *dhamma* can irreversibly shift the culture and civilization of the planet for all beings.

The Magical Path to AWE

Now I am creating the awakened life,
Of wise vision, intention, speech, and action
Living mindfully, with goodwill, loving all beings
With right livelihood and four wholesome efforts
Devoted to *dana, sila, samadhi,* and *panna!*

Ending ignorance and suffering
Unbinding from the habits of
Doubt and fear, greed, and hate
Delusions of ego and material desires of six senses
Seeing five aggregates as *anitya, dukkha, anatta*

No longer confusing making merit, ritual
and external refuge as the way
To cleanse one's mind, body, speech habits
Not staying blind, doing harm by willful ignorance
It's dark fruit of repeated pain and deadly inheritance

By resolving to wake up from all fake views in this life
Turning inward into the cave of the One sacred heart
Opening the mind and inner sense gates
Becoming still, one pointed, equanimous, empty
One awakens to the unconditioned *nirvana!*

-This poem is inspired by The Magical Path by Marc Allen

Like many Bengali folks, my heart was immersed into the joyful radiant songs of the universal poet Rabindranath Tagore, the fearless spirit of Vivekananda, and my own mother's compassionate heart.

Where the Mind is without Fear

Where the mind is without fear, where the knowledge is free
Where the world has not been broken up into fragments
By narrow domestic walls

Where words come out from the depth of truth
Where tireless striving stretches its arms toward perfection
Where the clear stream of reason has not lost its way
Into the dreary desert sand of dead habits

Where the mind is led forward by thee
Into ever-widening thought and action
Into that heaven of freedom,
Let our *Planet* awake!

-Rabindranath Tagore (*italics mine*)

"The greatest religion is to be true to your own nature.
Have faith in yourself"
-Swami Vivekananda

Sangha of AWE Circles

"Never underestimate the power of a small group of
committed people to change the world. In fact,
it is the only thing that ever has."
-Margaret Mead, cultural anthropologist

"Do not avoid contact with suffering or close your eyes
before suffering. Do not lose awareness of the existence
of suffering in the life of the world. Find ways to be with
those who are suffering, including personal contact, visits,
images, and sounds. By such means, awaken yourself and
others to the reality of suffering in the world. Nonviolent

action, born of the awareness of suffering and nurtured
by love, is the most effective way to confront adversity."
                    -Thich Nhat Hanh

Dharma in the West brings many challenges, which are also opportunities in disguise. Personally, I had to face discrimination both in my job from the manager and bullying in the sangha from a senior teacher and director. Navigating gender, power, culture, and social dynamics as an immigrant woman of color was hard. It is not easy to speak up when you are new, wanting to belong, and unsure of your place in a mostly white or a sharply divided black and white world.

After hearing the phrase "cultural baggage" of traditional (Asian) Buddhists a few times in a university chautauqua lecture by a well-known Buddhist scholar, I mustered enough courage to stand up and pose the question, "I just wonder what the baggage of the converted Buddhists looks like to you, since it is easy to see the fault of others and not our own." I remember having a good light-hearted talk with the speaker as he poked fun at himself for his mistake. One thing spiritual practitioners of all colors and cultures must not forget is that our intentional actions (sometimes non-action and negligence) through body, mind, and speech creates *karma*. There is power in kindness and wise speech.

After the Buddha and the *dharma*, *sangha* is the third jewel we take refuge into as support for our mindfulness practice. It is the most challenging and also most fulfilling refuge on the path of *dharma*. Even Buddha needed a *sangha* to plant the tree of *dharma* wide and deep. It continues even after 2,600 years through many cultures in many traditions and lineages. The voice of the feminine and mother lineage and marginalized groups have been missing from the *dharma* for too long. Women and minorities can come together to create and build the inclusive and resilient healing spaces needed for strongly rooted sanghas here in the West.

> "A (true) sangha is a community of friends practicing the dharma together in order to bring about and maintain awareness. The essence of a sangha is awareness, understanding, acceptance, harmony, and love. When you do not see these in a community, it is not a true sangha, and you should have the courage to say so. But when you find these elements are present in a community, you know that you have the happiness and fortune of being in a real sangha."
>
> -Thich Naht Hahn

Apply for a free forum membership as the leader of an AWE Circle at your workplace, home, or neighborhood. Get resources and support as they become available by visiting susmitabarua.com.

Reflections on a vision for the planet

> "Vision without action is lame, action without vision is a nightmare."
>
> -A Japanese Proverb

> "Sacred activism is a transforming force of compassion-in-action that is born of a fusion of deep spiritual knowledge, courage, love, and passion with wise radical action in the world."
>
> -Andrew Harvey

"We cannot solve our problems with the same thinking we used when we created them."
-Albert Einstein

"You never change things by fighting the existing reality. To change something, build a new model that makes the existing model obsolete."
-Buckminster Fuller

Spontaneous engagements

After my spontaneous awakening in August 1993, I was immersed in an inner world of deep exploration, sometimes almost in a twilight zone, so to speak, for almost seven years. I started feeling an inner restlessness around 1999 and the need to connect with the world through the internet. In three days, I built my spiritual website (without any training) to share my philosophy and journey for the benefit of all in early 2001, before the events of 9-11 the same year.

I now know not to ignore these occasional heart tremors, vibrations, and sacred signals coming from the universal energetic field. In those moments, I am driven to take spontaneous action far beyond my comfort zone. These actions are inspired by synchronicity of random events. These may include a talk or workshop in front of strangers and new groups like the US Social Forum II, organize a peace rally for the World March for Peace 2009, or longer engagements like volunteering for women's prison, local hospice, advocacy for *bhikkhunis* as the President of Alliance for Bhikkhunis, host meetup mindful dialogue group, write blogs and online articles for Tikkun, Global Justice movement, Global fund for women and such, inspired by open invitation or by some important geo-political-economic events.

Effects of awakening

I was aware of many subtle physiological adjustments and internal rewiring of some sort for many years after my awakening. My whole brain-body became more sensitive, alert and opened to multiple channels of information. It was sometimes chaotic and disturbing. Sometimes, I would be compelled to write down many pages to capture some of my thoughtstream coming like a flood. I would experience sudden tingling, expansion, and pressure in certain parts of the stomach, face, mouth, inner ear, heart, and brain. I might lose awareness of time and day for extended periods, unbounded expansive states along with strange sensations and symptoms that would come and go and rarely felt the need to see doctors.

A powerful vision for the planet appeared in my consciousness which I shared on my website and over 100K+ people visited my website and blog in the first 15 years from all over the world. I had no idea how to manifest it except I was very passionately engaged in connecting with all positive and peaceful initiatives that came to my wise attention online. My only compensation was the great joy and happiness I felt seeing every co-creative initiative big and mostly small. In my planning job I felt that the whole planet is going the wrong way, and somehow, I must be the change I want to see in the world. Following is the vision I wrote for the New Earth Paradigm in February, 2001 in my first website seek2know.net (that domain was lost)..

The New Earth Paradigm

I. Promote the spirit of open-minded free inquiry in all areas of human endeavors including awareness-based alternative-integrative-holistic and non-dual quantum approaches to self-knowledge, medicine, healing, education, science, technology, architecture, environment, space, performing arts, psychology, religion, forms of organization, work, recreation, mindful life, and living;

II. Pursue true freedom of choice in all human knowledge, thought and actions with responsibility and realize the highest human ideals, aspirations, and potentials in ways that honor and serve all life on the planet.

III. Co-Create a vibrant network of intentional communities among all forward thinking, positive and constructive initiatives that are taking shape at the local, regional, national, and global level; such organic and spontaneous initiatives will create a new vision and ultimately a grand human experience for all to participate in by receiving and giving freely!

Free and open inquiry is the basis for the scientific method and all other modes of investigation that produce, expand, and refine knowledge. Inquiry based learning allows many points of views, uncovers fixed views and dogmas, and then arrives at the right understanding and wise vision. Intentions are like seeds of creation planted in consciousness and then nurtured and acted for the intended values and long-term benefits in future.

Intentions that arise from pure-heart *bodhicitta* or awakened mind are far more impactful in the long run than goals from ordinary unenlightened minds, because they carry high frequency energy coming from beyond the physical dimension.

"With the insight into our profound interrelatedness you know that actions undertaken with pure intent have repercussions throughout the web of life, beyond what you can measure or discern."
-Choegyal Rinpoche

The paradigms of racism, sexism, patriarchy, sectarianism, colonialism, capitalism, imperialism along with generational trauma, marginalization of minorities and women would collapse with growing awareness and wisdom of open inquiry, radical honesty, courage, deep listening, self-love, self-acceptance, and self-compassion.

What this means for you: As a leader of your own life and livelihood, see where you can stretch a little more to live the most inspiring version of yourself this year. Celebrate your own practice of Awakening With Ease (AWE) process and support others in their journey to healing and wholeness. Everything we need to overcome personally and collectively, locally, and globally, begins and ends with awareness.

"Whatever precious jewel there is in the heavenly worlds, there is nothing comparable to one who is awakened."
-The Buddha, Sutta Nipata

"The gift of dharma surpasses all gifts,
The taste of dharma surpasses all tastes.
The delight of dharma surpasses all delight,
The ending of craving conquers all suffering."
-Dhammapada 24:354

*"Though one may conquer a thousand times a thousand
men in battle, yet he indeed is the noblest victor,
who conquers himself.*
-Dhammapada 3:103

Here conquering oneself means, conquering one's own ignorance. For me this process for Awakening With Ease (AWE)
began by turning the senses and attention inward, asking
deep questions about self-identity, nature of mind, reality
from universal view, listening to the inner voice, remembering
the direct experiences of unbounded awareness, joy and sad-
ness, early epiphanies, sacred site travels, lucid dreams and
sustaining loving awareness by unplugging from the past
hurts and future worries. Your own inner power to wake up
lies close to your deepest inquiries informed by your trauma,
pain, and suffering.

Just like the Buddha, we can become our own healer by taking
our own warrior's journey to ultimate peace and liberation
from illusion and ignorance. Just falling asleep by repeating
the three jewels of the Buddha, *dhamma,* and *sangha* gave
me the courage, wisdom, and strength to discover, walk and
remember the ancient *ariya* path of the noble ones on my
own. You can, too. Trust in the truth of the *dhamma* builds in
small increments, drop by drop, moment by moment.

Guardians of true *dharma*

"Heedfulness is the path to the Deathless
Heedlessness the path to death,
The mindful do not die
The heedless are as if already dead.
Knowing this distinction

The wise rejoice in heedfulness
Delighting
In the field of Noble Ones"
-Dhammapada 2:21-22

COVID-19 is a clear wake up call to the collective psyche of the people and the planet. The whole world is burning with social, economic, political, and climate urgency, crisis in leadership and uncertainty. The old-world structures and systems based on unrestrained forces of greed, hate, control, and delusion are crumbling. Learn to nurture healing love, inner peace, self-compassion, mindful living, creativity, right action, right use of power, spiritual community, friendship, and collaboration to manifest our collective vision based on wise understanding of things as they are.

The Buddha pointed out in many ways that one's conduct is what defines one's value, worth and noble status according to right understanding and practice of true *dharma*, and not by one's birth, color, caste, class, beauty or gender, or any human constructs of hierarchy. He pinpointed sixty-two commonly held views by ascetics in his time around the self, nature, and the Gods. He felt many were caught up in a 'net of views,' secular and religious, upon which people built up an identity. By standing outside this net of views, he discovered the way to final release from suffering of *samsara* (Brahmajala Sutta, DN1). The guardians of true *dharma* are the noble ones, who must be recognized, supported, and respected by the four-fold monastic and lay *sangha of noble men and women.*

"What are all these titles and races?
They are a mere name."
-Buddha, SN 648

"True teachings (*dhamma*) are like true gold, which doesn't disappear (goes out of use) as long as counterfeit gold hasn't appeared in the world. But when counterfeit gold appears in the world then real gold disappears. In the same way, the true teaching doesn't disappear as long the counterfeit of the true teaching hasn't appeared in the world. But when the counterfeit of the true teaching appears in the world then the true teaching disappears. True *dhamma* does not disappear through natural calamities, but by the arising of foolish unwise people (who grasp at wrong views, having little reverence and respect for the enlightened teacher, the true teachings, the noble sangha, the right training, and meditation) right amidst the *sangha*."

–Saddhamma Patirupaka Sutta (SN 16.13)

To birth a new culture of awakening and enlightened society, be the change you want to see and walk the way of a peaceful warrior, who conquers his own ignorance, anger, pain, and fear. With love, nurture the seeds of aliveness, joy, inquiry, energetic effort, and inspiration that are within you. Know your inherent worth and all the gifts you have already received in this precious human birth. You are born to discover the heart's path to fearless peace and freedom from ignorance. Experience the bliss of natural awakening process through open awareness, cultivate wise view, attention, intention, speech, and action serving the well-being of your authentic alive self, people, and planet.

AWE circles

This book is a guide to essential Dhamma. Clarity of vision and intention in daily and weekly practice creates the right direction, energy and momentum on the path. Having spiritual friends is the whole of holy path of practice.

> "Those who consider the inessential to be essential
> And see the essential as inessential
> Don't reach the essential,
> Living in the field of wrong intention.
>
> Those who know the essential to be essential,
> And the inessential as inessential
> Reach the essential,
> Living in the field of right intention."
>
> -Dhammapada 1:11-12

Imagine yourself and each person reading and practicing the six principles in this book, becoming a point of light in many spontaneous study and practice of AWE Circles around the planet.

AWE Circles are based on the cultivation of admirable spiritual friendship (*kalyana mittata*) and loving-kindness (*metta*). According to the Buddha, the first criteria for attaining the wings of awakening is to have good spiritual friends of conviction, virtue, generosity, and wisdom. He also said associating with such wise friends—who are with you in happiness and sorrow and who care for your well-being and happiness—is not only a part but the "whole of spiritual life."

Start an AWE Circle in your home, work, or community today!

Begin with one to three friends and let each one bring a friend. Make a commitment to study, discuss and practice together for six months to one year. Develop new habits of listening and speaking from the heart and meditating together for happiness, inner peace, and freedom. Right view is the forerunner of right intention, speech, action, livelihood, effort, and mindfulness. Practice right speech by abstaining from lying, from divisive speech, from abusive speech, and from idle chatter (gossip). The five keys to right speech are: "It is spoken at the right time. It is spoken in truth. It is spoken affectionately. It is spoken beneficially. It is spoken with a mind of goodwill." (AN 5.198)

Purity of heart-mind and conduct creates an energetic field that attracts well-being and blessings to all who are receptive to the energy of concord and well-being. The mental defilements, animosity, and victimhood in our daily attitudes also manifest as pollution in our natural and social environment. Most of us do not pay attention to our ruminating thoughts, pulling us into the past hurts and projecting the same onto the future. If we want to change our reality, we need to change our core beliefs and limitations (repetitive thoughts) with empowering thoughts. Our bodies are listening to every fearful thought and judgments about the past, present, and future. Love and bless everyone you meet, including yourself while looking in the mirror.

The Buddha gave this simile to describe the situation of ordinary uninstructed people (puthujjana): Like a dog on a leash, there is no making an end to suffering for beings who are roaming and wandering hindered by ignorance and fettered by sensual craving. The dog-leash is tied around a post made of the five aggregates of form, feeling, perception, mental habits, and consciousness.

Cutting identification with this post as "I, me, mine" (wrong-view) and unbinding from this would gradually lead to cessation of the links of dependent origination (this-that conditionality). Avoiding both the extremes of sensual self-indulgence and sensual self-denial Tathagata (Buddha) realized the Middle Way—producing vision, producing knowledge—leads to calm, to direct knowledge, to self-awakening, to unbinding, to the freedom of the unconditioned, deathless, *nibbana*.

> Just remember this, especially when you see abuse of power on the part of a dhamma teacher or leadership council while developing or being part of a AWE circle or Sangha.

> "Don't give up your own welfare
> For the sake of others' welfare, however great,
> Clearly know your own welfare
> And be intent on the highest good."
> -Dh 12:166

To embark on such a noble and profound endeavor to walk the path of awakening from ignorance and forgetfulness to knowledge and mindfulness, all you need is here in this book. Just remember your childhood innocence, desire to know, curiosity, wonder, imagination, adventure, and trust here and now. See the goodness in children and adults you met today. See all things with a fresh beginner's mind, even if you are seeing it for the one hundredth time. You will not get lonely, addicted, depressed, or cynical about the world and your own worth. See yourself as, *I am enough, I have enough, and I do enough.* Let go of the habit of lack, scarcity, and insecurity about being worthy and deserving for a day or even an hour for a change.

Begin fresh with a beginner's mind, trust your own goodness, and resolve to go beyond doubt, transcend self-view and end suffering by ending ignorance. Have confidence in *buddhadharma*. Just that is enough. Instead of stress and despair, learn to be still, ask, and wait. Listen to the soft whisper of your inner guide, guru, and teacher. Look for signs and synchronicities in your inner or outer environment for the next right step.

"Those bhikkhus of mine, Ananda, who now or after I am gone, abide as an island unto themselves, as a refuge unto themselves, seeking no other refuge; having the Dhamma as their island and refuge, seeking no other refuge: it is they who will become the highest, if they have the desire to learn."
- last words of the Buddha.

"You can do anything you want to do. It's only your thought that you can't do it that holds you back."
-Dipama

"A mind unruffled by the vagaries of fortune, freed from sorrow, cleansed from defilements, liberated from fear - this is the highest blessing"
-Buddha, Mangala Sutta

We are living through unprecedented time of change, disruption, fear, and chaos on many levels now. Yet, it is also the time of great turning and transformation when the energy of creativity, innovation, partnership, peaceful collaboration, and intentional community movements based on social-environmental awareness, love, wisdom, and compassion have the potential to come in full swing in next fifty years. Wise attention to living each day from a mindful conscious paradigm of doing no harm, doing good and intentionally raise our mental vibration could help whole communities to awaken with ease.

Letting go of the old habitual patterns of fear, blame, shame, control, anger, division, conflict, and narrow identity-based politics is crucial now to make the clear shift towards conscious evolution of love, loving action and choosing the right use of resources and worldly power will be in front of us. The rhythm and vibration of Universal Truth (Dhamma Chanda) is naturally built within the collective intelligence of wholesome human mind, healthy body, right speech, and action. Living from this higher frequency energy of love, generosity, virtue, and fearless compassion will keep the energy of abundance in flow and make us ride through rough times.

> "Do everything with a mind that lets go. If you let go a little, you will have a little peace. If you let go a lot, you will have a lot of peace. If you let go completely, you will have complete peace. Your struggle in this world will have come to an end."
>
> -Ajahn Chah, Thai Buddhist Master

> ""The entire spiritual journey rests on the morality of non-harming. This is the expression of the love and care we feel both for others and for ourselves."
>
> -Joseph Goldstein, One Dharma

Thank you for reading this far. I appreciate your time, trust, and sincerity to open your mind to new knowledge and practice. The experience of meditative stillness or Jhana comes naturally to a mind inwhich faith, virtue and sense-restraint have been cultivated and developed, where hindrances have been suppressed and purity of mind has been developed with loving-kindness and compassion toward all beings and mindful-awareness has been developed.

The more you are aware of the refined, subtle and beautiful part of your mind, the closer your mind is in accessing dhamma. Your deeper mind is already inclined towards universal knowledge and knowing the freedom, happiness and peace of Nibbana. As Ajahn Brahm says, "Nibbana is only hidden behind the thinnest of veils." Set your intention to go beyond self-view, doubt and clinging to precepts and practices.

"Don't ask what the world needs. Ask what makes you come alive, and go do it. Because what the world needs is people who have come alive."
-Howard Thurman

Your practice will flow well with a sense of aliveness, joy and ease. When you rejoice in the good deed and qualities of others, their success, intelligence, happiness, and well-being, you will feel genuine happiness and sympathetic joy (mudita) for them. Buddha said, a joyful mind is easily concentrated. The wisdom of equanimity is the fruit of meditative life and the hallmark of compassionate leaders, peace-makers and noble citizens. Outside conditions will only change to the degree our inner dialogue, thinking, perception, worldview, paradigms, ideas, visions, intentions, words, actions and livelihood are consciously motivated by universal loving-kindness, ethics of non-harm, and compassion for all beings. Use your status, wealth, privilege and power to be an ally and spiritual friend for those who are marginalized and abused by the system.

> *"I learned this, at least, by my experiment; that if one advances confidently in the direction of his dreams, and endeavors to live the life which he has imagined, he will meet with a success unexpected in common hours. He will put some things behind, will pass an invisible boundary; ... and he will live with the license of a higher order of beings."*
>
> *-Henry David Thoreau, Walden*

The Buddha said, in the universe, it is rare and difficult to be born as human; difficult is the life of mortals, it is rare to come across the true teachings of Dhamma, and difficult is the arising of buddhas. So we all need make best use of our precious human birth. If I can be of any help or support on your mindful path and journey to total health, healing, purpose, and wholeness, please reach out to me or a person on my team. Do the same for any mindful collaboration, event, or partnership that is related to the front cover of this book, no matter where you are in the world. Connect with me at awakeneasy.com, susmitabarua.com or Acharya Susmita Barua on LinkedIn. Remember, to do no harm, to cultivate good, and to cleanse one's mind — this is the teaching of the Buddhas.

Bibliography

Allen, Marc. *The Magical Path: Creating the Life of Your Dreams and a World That Works for All.* New World Library, 2012.

Banks, Elizabeth. *Who the Hell is Maslow, and What Are His Theories All About?* Bowden & Brazil, 2022

Barua, Susmita. "Magical Moments with Maya"; *Pearls of Wisdom: A Second Strand,* compiled by Patricia Crane and Rick Nichols. The Crane's Nest, 2006, p. 134.

Barua, Susmita. "Igniting the Inner Coach, Light Body to Awaken Self." *The Power of Life Coaching.* vol. 2, edited by Barbara Wainwright, Balboa Press, 2018.

Barua, Susmita. "Bridging Science and Spirituality Through Buddha's Middle Way to Knowledge." *Teaching Dhamma in New Lands,* The 2nd International Association of Buddhist Universities (IABU) Conference, MCU, Ayutthaya, Thailand, 2012.

Barua, Susmita. "A Buddhist and Interfaith Response to Debt-Capitalism." *Tikkun.Org Online Magazine,* 2015.

Bodhi, Bhikkhu. *The Buddha's Teachings on Social and Communal Harmony: An Anthology of Discourses from the Pali Canon.* Wisdom Publications, 2016.

Braden, Gregg. *The Inner Technology of Prayer: Tuning Oneself to the Creative Forces of the Universe.* Audiobook by Sounds True, 2011.

Brahm, Ajahn. *Mindfulness, Bliss, and Beyond: A Meditator's Handbook.* Wisdom Publications, 2006.

Brown, Brene. *Dare to Lead: Brave Work, Tough Conversations, Whole Hearts.* Random House, 2018.

Einstein, Albert. *Einstein on Cosmic Religion and Other Opinions and Aphorisms.* Dover Publications, 2009.

Fronsdal, Gil. *The Dhammapada: A New Translation of the Buddhist Classic with Annotations.* Shambhala Publications, 2006.

Goldstein, Joseph. *One Dharma: The Emerging Western Buddhism.* HarperOne, 2003.

Hawkins, David R. *Power vs. Force: The Hidden Determinants of Human Behavior.* Hay House, 2002.

Kornfield, Jack. *The Wise Heart: A Guide to the Universal Teachings of Buddhist Psychology.* Bantam Books, Random House, 2009.

Maxwell, John C. *Developing the Leader Within You 2.0.* Harper Collins Leadership, 2019.

Mitchel, Stephen. *Tao Te Ching: A New English Version (Perennial Classics).* Harper Perennial, Modern Classics, 2006.

Pueblo, Yung. *Clarity and Connection.* Andrew McMeel Publishing, 2021.

Shute, Scott. *Full Body Yes: Change Your Work and Your World from Inside Out.* Ingram, 2021.

Tharoor, Sashi. *The Inglorious Empire: What the British Did to India.* Scribe, 2017.

Ware, Bonnie. *Top Five Regrets of The Dying: A Life Transformed by the Dearly Departing.* Hay House, 2019.

Early Buddhist Texts (Abbreviations) in Pali

Anguttara Nikaya (AN)
Digha Nikaya (DN)
Majjhima Nikaya (MN)
Samyutta Nikaya (SN)
Khuddaka Nikaya (KN)

Other minor collections are Kuddhakapāṭha (Kp), Dhammapada (Dhp), Udāna (Ud), Itivuttaka (Iti), Sutta Nipāta (Snp), Vimānavatthu (Vv), Petavatthu (Pv), Theragāthā (Thag), and Therīgāthā (Thig)

There are parallel texts called Agamas in Chinese.

Online Sources of Early Buddhist Text (EBT)

Suttacentral @https://www.suttacentral.net for more complete text abbreviations and descriptions in English and other languages, initiated by Bhanre Sujato, Bhante

Brahmali, and others in Australia. It has an active Discuss and Discover Forum.

Access to Insight @https://www.accesstoinsight.org has selected suttas and parallel translations contributed by various monasteries in the UK, US, and Sri Lanka.

Buddhist Publication Society, Sri Lanka @https://www.bps.lk/library.php

The Open Buddhist University @https://www.buddhistuniversity.net is an unaccredited, digital resource run by Khemarato Bhikkhu since 2020.

Daily Sutta Study @https://Readingfaithfully.org and https://Pariyatti.org

Dharma audio and video recordings

@Abhayagiri.org; @Anukampaproject.org;
@Audiodharma.org
@Bhikkhuni.net/library; @Buddhistinsights.org;
@Buddhistinquiry.org
@Clearmountainmonastery.org; @Dhammadharini.net;
@Dhammatalks.org; @Dharma-documentaries.net;
@Dharmaseed.org; @Dougsdharma.com; @Sati.org;
@Spiritrock.org; @Youtube.com

www.ingramcontent.com/pod-product-compliance
Lightning Source LLC
LaVergne TN
LVHW051504080426
835509LV00017B/1907